WITNESS

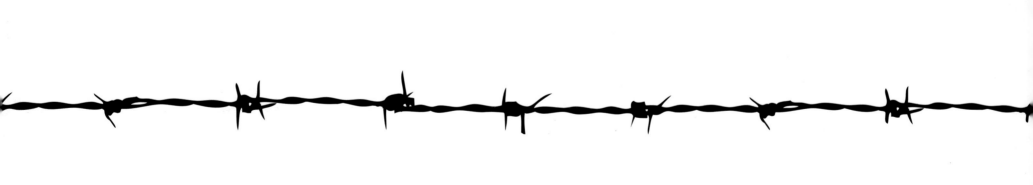

WITNESS

PASSING THE TORCH OF HOLOCAUST MEMORY TO NEW GENERATIONS

Compiled by
Eli Rubenstein with
March of the Living

Second Story Press

Library and Archives Canada Cataloguing in Publication

Rubenstein, Eli, 1959-, compiler
Witness : passing the torch of Holocaust memory to new generations / compiled by Eli Rubenstein.

ISBN 978-1-927583-66-1 (bound).—ISBN 978-1-927583-89-0 (paperback)

1. Holocaust, Jewish (1939-1945)—Personal narratives. 2. Holocaust, Jewish (1939-1945)—Pictorial works.
3. Holocaust survivors—Travel—Poland. 4. Jewish youth—Travel—Poland.
5. March of the Living (Organization). I. Title.

D804.3.R82 2015   940.53'180922   C2014-908138-3

Edited by Carolyn Jackson
Copyedited by Phuong Truong
Designed by Melissa Kaita

Printed and bound in China

*Second Story Press gratefully acknowledges the support of the Ontario Arts Council and the
Canada Council for the Arts for our publishing program. We acknowledge the financial support
of the Government of Canada through the Canada Book Fund.*

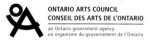

Published by
SECOND STORY PRESS
20 Maud Street, Suite 401
Toronto, ON M5V 2M5
www.secondstorypress.ca

TABLE OF CONTENTS

INTERACTIVE BOOK

View Survivor Testimony from the Archives of USC Shoah Foundation and March of the Living

To Scan and View Videos:
Download the free *Digimarc Discover* app on your smartphone or other device and scan images that carry the blue flame icon to unlock exclusive stories from survivors of the Holocaust.

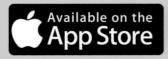
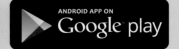

MESSAGE FROM HIS HOLINESS, POPE FRANCIS

I ask you to convey to the organizers of the March of Living my closeness to them and their mission. All the efforts for fighting in favor of life are praiseworthy and have to be supported without any kind of discrimination. For this reason I am very close to these initiatives, that are not only against death but also against the thousands discriminatory phobias that enslave and kill.

I thank them for all their doings, and pray to the Lord a blessing for them in this struggle for life, equality and dignity.

…le pido a Usted que haga llegar a los organizadores de la Marcha por la Vida mi cercanía. Todo esfuerzo por luchar a favor de la vida es loable y se debe apoyar sin ningún tipo de discriminación. Por este motivo estoy cercano a estas iniciativas que van no sólo contra la muerte sino también contra las mil y una fobias discriminatorias que esclavizan y matan. Les agradezco todo lo que hacen y pido al Señor que los bendiga en esta lucha a favor de la vida, de la igualdad y la dignidad.

Cordialmente,

His Holiness Pope Francis
The Vatican
Rome, Italy

DEAR READER,

As one of the founders of the March of the Living program over a quarter of a century ago, little did I realize the exceptional impact the program would have in the ensuing years. Since that first journey in 1988, more than 200,000 people – presidents and prime ministers, community leaders and religious figures, teachers and chaperones, students and survivors – have joined this life-changing experience.

All are to be commended for traveling to Auschwitz-Birkenau, the place that symbolizes the very abyss of humanity, to commit to building a world free of hate, prejudice, and genocide. Indeed, many have returned to their homes to become become important agents for positive change within their communities.

But of course, it is the Holocaust survivors – the voices of our past – and the students – the custodians of our future – who deserve the most praise.

We have the utmost admiration for the survivors, who courageously share their difficult stories, even though each telling brings back memories of a dark era, beyond our imagination to comprehend. We are forever grateful to them for entrusting their stories with the next generation.

And to the young students, thank you for agreeing to carry the torch of memory for the survivors, to be "the witnesses for the witnesses."

As you leaf through the pages of this book, I would like you to notice this: there is not one poem, not one quote, not one statement, that promotes anger, hatred, or revenge – not one expression of bitterness. This is a true testament of the character of the survivors and students who take part in this remarkable journey.

Anne Frank taught us "How wonderful it is that nobody need wait a single moment before starting to improve the world."

As you observe the images and the texts from over a quarter of a century of the March of the Living, I ask each one of you to decide how you are going to change the world, how you are going to honor the legacy of the survivors. Take a moment to pause and reflect and make a silent pledge to yourself to do your part in the fight for justice and equality.

And after you finish reading the work, please continue to carry with you the message of the March of the Living, a message that proclaims that the world must finally rid itself of all forms of anti-Semitism and racism, that all human beings deserve dignity and equality, and that a tragedy like the Holocaust must never be allowed to happen again, at any time, in any place, to any people.

Dr. Shmuel Rosenman
Founder & Chairman, March of the Living International

INTRODUCTION

In the history of humanity, replete with wars, massacres, and wanton destruction, the Holocaust stands out among the darkest stains on our morally fractured past. In the first half of the 20th century, German achievements in music, art, literature, philosophy, and science epitomized the height of Western civilization, yet this was the nation that singled out for eradication an entire people in the most horrifying manner. And it very nearly succeeded.

But Nazi Germany did not target Jews alone. Members of other minorities and innocent populations – Poles, Roma, Soviet POWs, the disabled, homosexuals, and many other groups – were viciously persecuted or slaughtered en masse.

Since the fall of Communism in 1989, more than 200,000 young people, accompanied by Holocaust survivors, have traveled to Poland and other parts of Europe on programs like March of the Living and March of Remembrance and Hope to study the history of the Holocaust and other WWII genocides perpetrated by Nazi Germany on millions of innocent victims.

Anne Frank, one of the most famous victims of the Holocaust, wrote, while still in hiding: "In spite of everything, I still believe that people are really good at heart." To which (pre-war) camp survivor Bruno Bettelheim responded, "If all men are good at heart, there never really was an Auschwitz."

How does one comprehend the enormity of the Holocaust? How can we understand the appalling cruelty that Nazi Germany and its collaborators exhibited? How do we preserve our young people's innocent belief in the goodness of humanity in the grim face of Auschwitz? Should we? In fact, does the Holocaust not teach us that humanity is inherently evil? And if humanity is so utterly hopeless, so beyond salvation, why should we care one whit about each other?

We may never have a definitive answer as to *why* the Holocaust took place. But we do know *how* to respond. The answers resound in the pages of this book.

The photos and quotes in this book emanate from two similar but distinct programs: March of the Living and March of Remembrance and Hope.

The **March of the Living** brings high school students, the majority of whom are Jewish, from all over the world to Poland to visit once thriving sites of Jewish life and culture, as well as Holocaust-related sites. On Holocaust Remembrance Day, the students march from Auschwitz to Birkenau in memory of all victims of Nazi genocide and against prejudice, intolerance, and hate. Some groups travel to Israel, after their experience in Poland.

The **March of Remembrance and Hope** is aimed at university students of all religions and backgrounds. Its purpose is to teach about the dangers of intolerance through the study of the Holocaust and other WWII genocides. The trip includes a short visit to Germany, followed by a longer visit to Poland, including many of the same sites as March of the Living.

On both programs, Holocaust survivors share the memory of their war-time experiences with the young people in the very places where they unfolded.

Image after image, story after story, statement after statement attest to the commitment of both survivors and students to build a world far different from the one Hitler sought to shape.

The Nazis wanted to build a world founded on hatred. We will build a world based on love. The Nazis wanted to use race, religion, and culture to divide people. We will accept and celebrate the diverse religions, races, and cultures that populate our world. The Nazis championed brute force and power. Our weapons will be kindness, compassion, and empathy. The Nazis descended to levels of inhumanity never before imagined. We will honor our common humanity.

There is a solution to the divide between Anne Frank and Bruno Bettelheim. Anne Frank, one may contend, was right for the most part. The majority of people are good at heart – but that is not nearly enough. We must also act, stand up, make a difference. Otherwise we become accomplices to the victimizers and, ultimately, enablers of Auschwitz. The Holocaust happened because of its twisted and evil perpetrators *and* because most of the world's good people did not stand up tall enough or soon enough.

To listen to the survivors and to act upon what they have learned – this is the commitment of the young people who embark on the challenging journeys reflected throughout this book. By doing so, the listeners become the tellers and, in the words of one young student after hearing a survivor's story, "the bearers of their memories."

Forever will I see the children who no longer have the strength to cry. Forever will I see the elderly who no longer have the strength to help them. Forever will I see the mothers and the fathers, the grandfathers and grandmothers, the little school children...their teachers...the righteous and the pious.... From where do we take the tears to cry over them? Who has the strength to cry for them?
—Elie Wiesel, March of the Living, 1990

CHAPTER ONE

WHAT HAPPENED? AND TO WHOM?

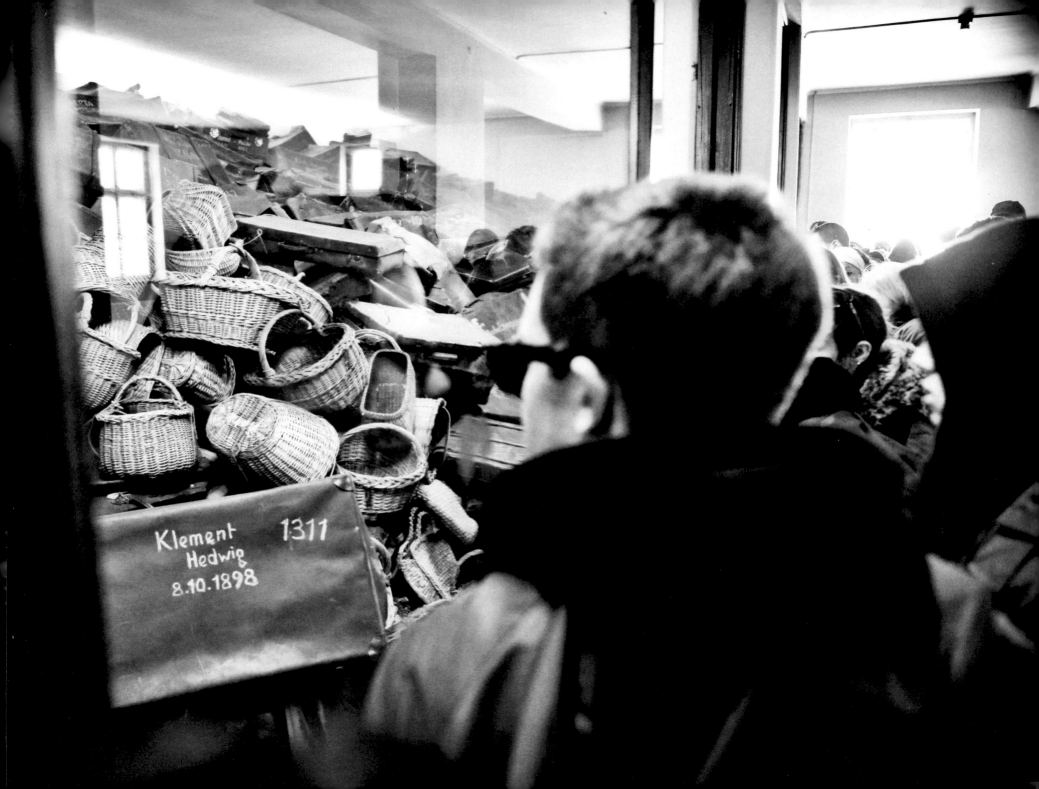

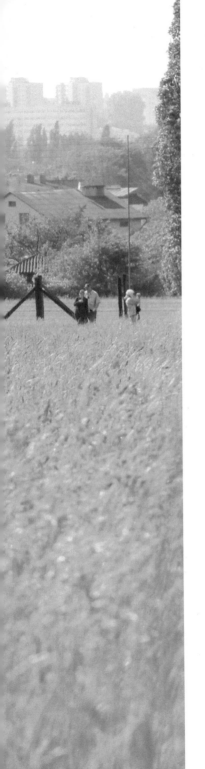

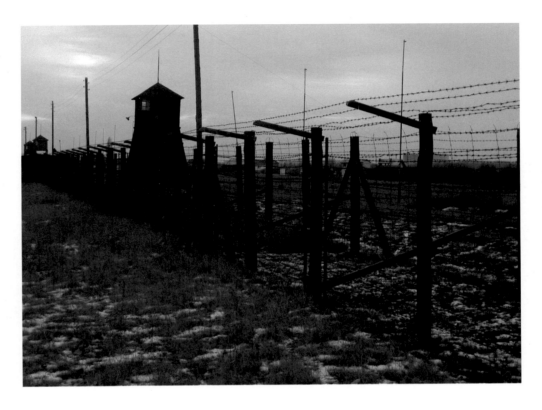

Approximately 80,000 people were murdered behind the barbed wire of the Majdanek camp.

Multi-faith university students on the March of Remembrance and Hope visit the barracks at Majdanek concentration camp, located on the outskirts of Lublin. Majdanek operated from October 1, 1941, until it was liberated in August 1944. The camp was used to kill people on an industrial scale at the same time as Operation Reinhard was being implemented.

25

Tragically, genocide has been perpetrated by the human race since the beginning of recorded history. The term was first coined by Rafael Lemkin, a Polish Jew whose many family members were murdered during the Holocaust. In his younger years, Lemkin was troubled by the intentional mass murder of Armenians by the Turks in 1915 and later by the slaughter of Christian Assyrians by Iraqis in 1933. After painstakingly documenting the brutal Nazi treatment of conquered populations throughout Europe in WWII, Lemkin dedicated his life to having the word *genocide* accepted – and to the need for the world community to ban its practice.

With the rise of Nazi Germany in 1933, human rights became its foremost victim. Many groups were targeted – government opposition, trade unionists, communists, homosexuals, Roma, and the disabled – but none were more vigorously pursued than the Jewish people, who alone were ultimately subjected to the goal of total annihilation.

CLASSICAL VS. MODERN ANTI-SEMITISM

It is important to distinguish among the various forms of classical anti-Semitism (or anti-Judaism) that existed over the centuries, modern anti-Semitism (more racial in tone), and Nazi racial ideology. Classical anti-Semitism was often based on theological positions, cultural stereotypes, fear of the Other, economic competition, superstitious beliefs, or combinations of the above. While these forms of anti-Semitism were never pleasant – and often resulted in violence and even murder – the goal was never the complete annihilation of the Jewish people. Further, the Jews usually had two "escape routes" – conversion or expulsion.

Nazi racial ideology built itself upon the more modern 19th century anti-Semitism, with its additional emphasis on alleged racial differences. To the Nazis, the Jews were doubly cursed. Their blood was tainted, and their values were emblematic of everything wrong in the world: equality, morality, democracy. The Nazis made it their mission to rescue the world from the perils of Western Civilization. Destroy the Jewish people and everything that Judaism represents (such as the theories of Einstein and Freud), and the world will be safe again. While initially this meant total removal of Jews from society, it developed into the goal of their total removal from the world.

The Nazis dramatically changed anti-Semitism into the belief that the redemption of the world relied on the

extermination of Jews from the face of the earth. *Only* extermination would do. While the Nazis did not invent racist anti-Semitism, they combined ancient and modern forms of anti-Semitism with their Nazi ideology to the point where they viewed the Jews as a dangerous race that threatened the existence of Germany and of the world.

To the German Nazis, the logical extension of their racial ideology was – eventually – the "Final Solution," whereby they forced large numbers of Jews into ghettos, organized mass-murdering death squads (such as the *Einsatzgruppen* and other police battalions and army units), built a network of death, concentration, and labor camps throughout Europe, and then transported the Jews to these camps, where most of them perished.

In addition to their war against the Jews, the Nazis committed war crimes against numerous other groups. An estimated two million Soviet POWs, 275,000 disabled, and up to 220,000 Roma were murdered by the Nazis. Other persecuted groups included homosexuals, political leftists, Jehovah's Witnesses, and many others with whom the Nazis found fault for various reasons.

THE MOST EXTREME FORM OF GENOCIDE

"The Holocaust," according to one writer, "has become the 'master narrative' for suffering, shaping discussions about every present conflict over genocide and human rights." Certainly, at first glance, there are aspects that seem to make the Holocaust stand out, even though each genocide is unique. The Holocaust is "uniquely, unique" as some have described it, not just because of the staggering number of victims, but also because of the machinery of death created by the Nazis in pursuit of their goal. They used modern technology to create assembly lines of death, where the "raw materials" were Jewish men, women, and children, and the "finished product" was ash (and side products of plundered Jewish possessions and gold teeth, hair etc.). The terrifying efficiency of this Nazi machine cannot but cause one to shudder and to recognize the level of ultimate evil to which humanity can descend.

Conceptually, too, the Holocaust was different from all other genocides. In mass murder, large numbers of people are killed by a government or other force; in genocide, mass murder takes place on an ongoing basis, with the goal of destroying the culture and/or national existence of another people. The Holocaust, however, was mass

murder and genocide…the attempt to annihilate the existence of an entire group of people, and obliterate it forever. What the Jews faced at the hands of the Nazis was unprecedented in human history.

What makes the Holocaust unique is the combination of three conditions: it was driven by ideological rather than pragmatic (land, resources etc.) reasons; it was global in reach; and the intended target was the entire Jewish people (from infancy to old age). "The Nazis were looking for Jews, for all Jews," in the words of eminent Holocaust historian Yehuda Bauer. As Dr. David Silberklang notes: "The very goal itself – a state plan to annihilate an entire people without exception, not to leave a single Jew alive under any circumstances – is what makes the Holocaust unique."

When one understands this, one comes face to face with the utter irrationality of the Holocaust, which maintained that the very redemption of the world relied upon the "extermination" of every last Jew, to finally and totally rid the world of this contemptible "virus." No course of action of any kind by the victim – supplication, conversion, bribery, slavery, or exile – could ever suffice or placate the Nazi agenda. No other mass murder or genocide was ever conceived or implemented on the basis of such an absolutist worldview.

In light of this, it has been argued that, on the continuum, the Holocaust is the most extreme form of genocide and should be the starting point of any attempt to understand genocide – not because Holocaust victims suffered more than others, but because of its unprecedented *and total* nature.

The Holocaust, perhaps more than any other genocide, teaches us – warns us – that lacking restraint, humanity's potential for extreme evil and cruelty is virtually without limit, beyond our worst fears and our wildest imagination.

Of course, the deaths of victims of mass murder, genocide, and the Holocaust are all unjust and must be mourned by the world community. As humanitarian Lieutenant-General Romeo Dallaire, former Canadian senator, reminds us: "No human is more human than any other." The victims of the various genocides throughout history may have perished for different reasons and under different circumstances – and this, indeed, is worthy of examination – but their lives were equally, infinitely, and immeasurably sacred.

Our study of all genocides should lead us to the acceptance of the fundamental equality of every member of the human family – their right to life, justice, freedom, and dignity – and the resolve to live together in peace.

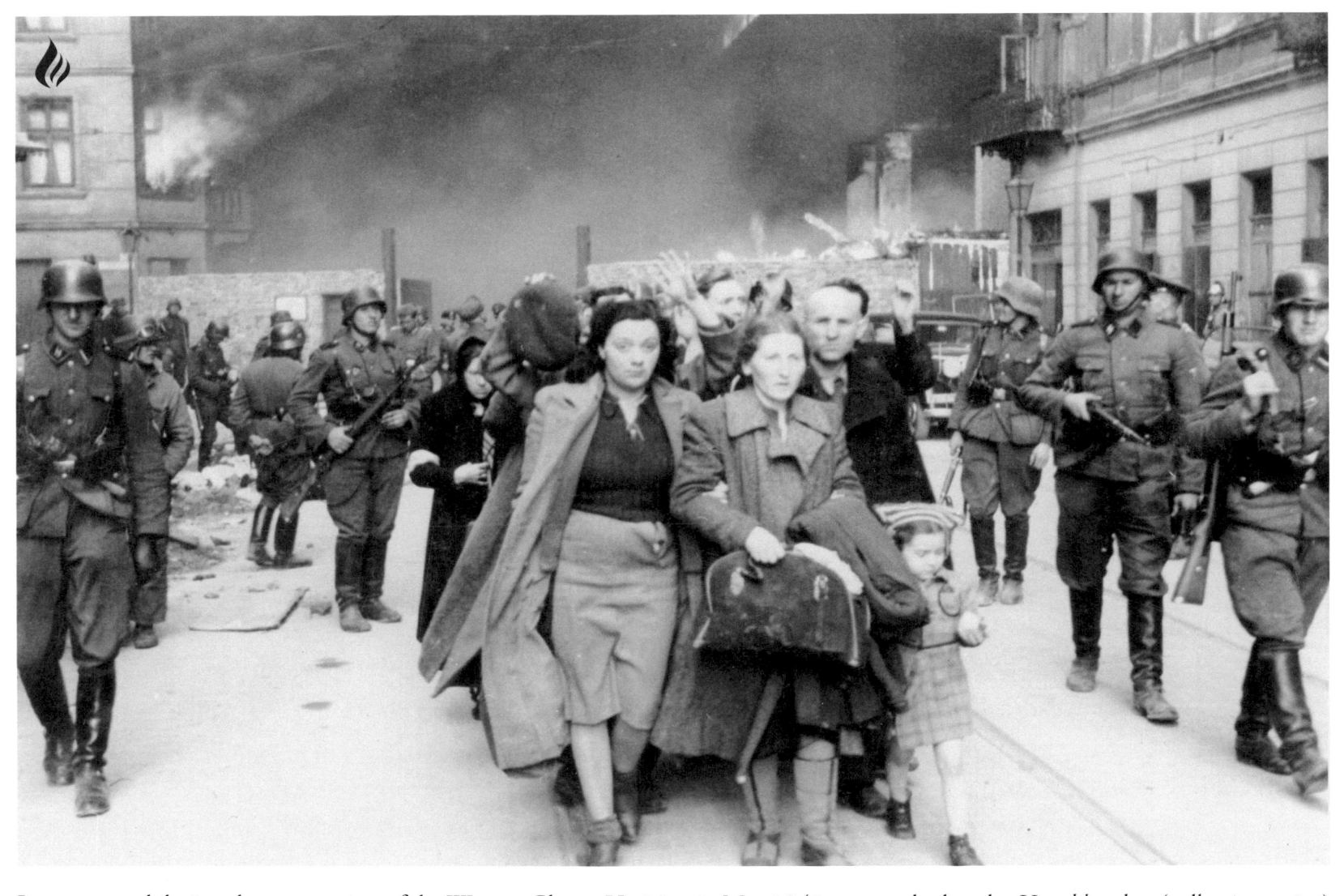

Jews captured during the suppression of the Warsaw Ghetto Uprising in May 1943 are marched to the *Umschlagplatz* (collection point) for deportation, many of them to Treblinka, where most of Warsaw's Jews met their end. Shortly after the German invasion of Poland in 1939, the Nazis began to corral Jews into ghettos, enclosed areas within cities throughout Eastern Europe. There were at least 1,000 ghettos in German-occupied and annexed Poland and the Soviet Union alone.

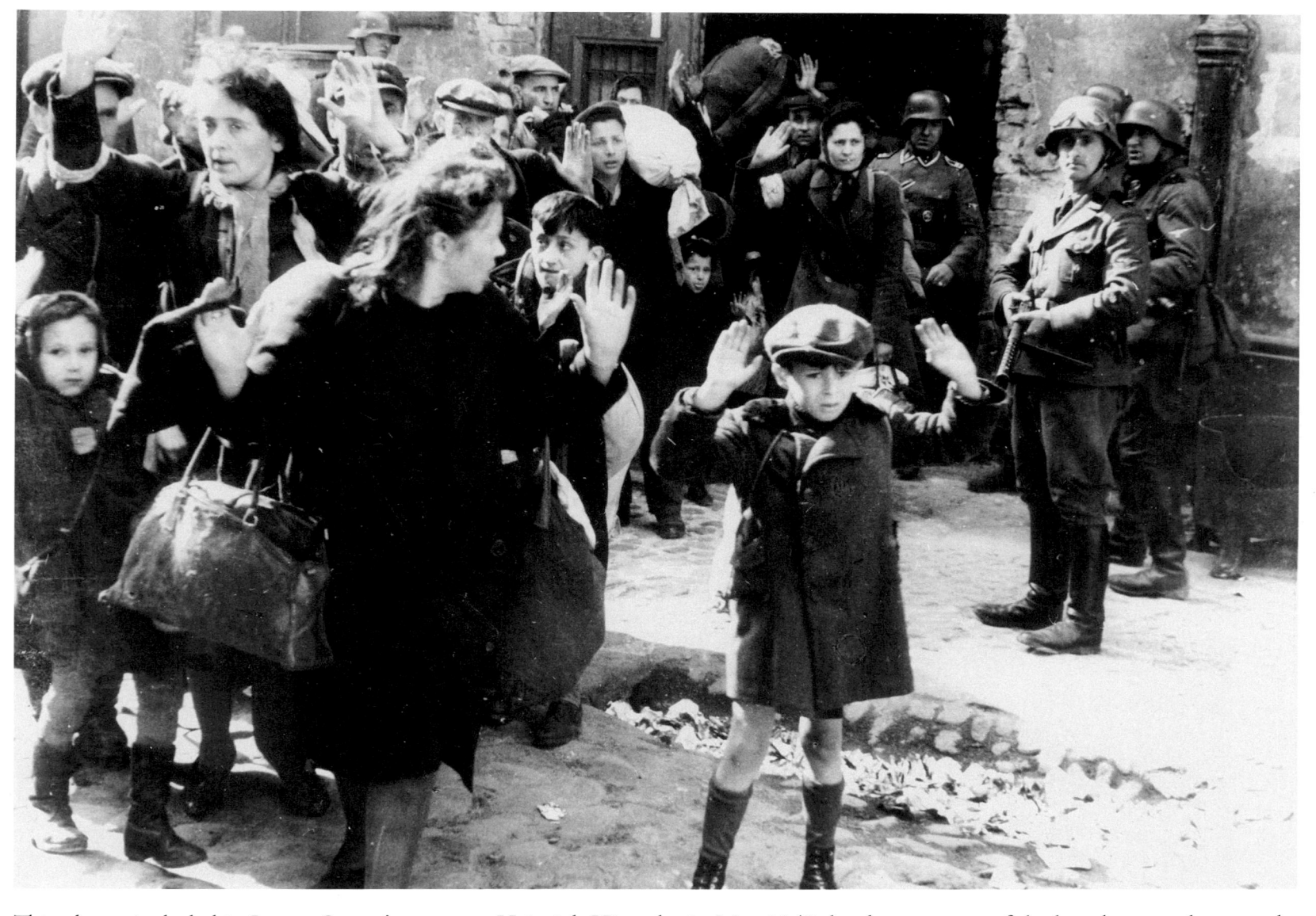

This photo, included in Jurgen Stroop's report to Heinrich Himmler in May 1943, has become one of the best-known photographs of World War II. The original German caption read: "Forcibly pulled out of dug-outs." The Warsaw Ghetto was aggressively cleared following the heroic Warsaw Ghetto Uprising, which lasted from April 19 to May 16, 1943. Conditions in the ghettos were extremely harsh and many died of disease, starvation, or were executed. All ghettos were eventually cleared, with the remaining Jews deported to concentration and extermination camps.

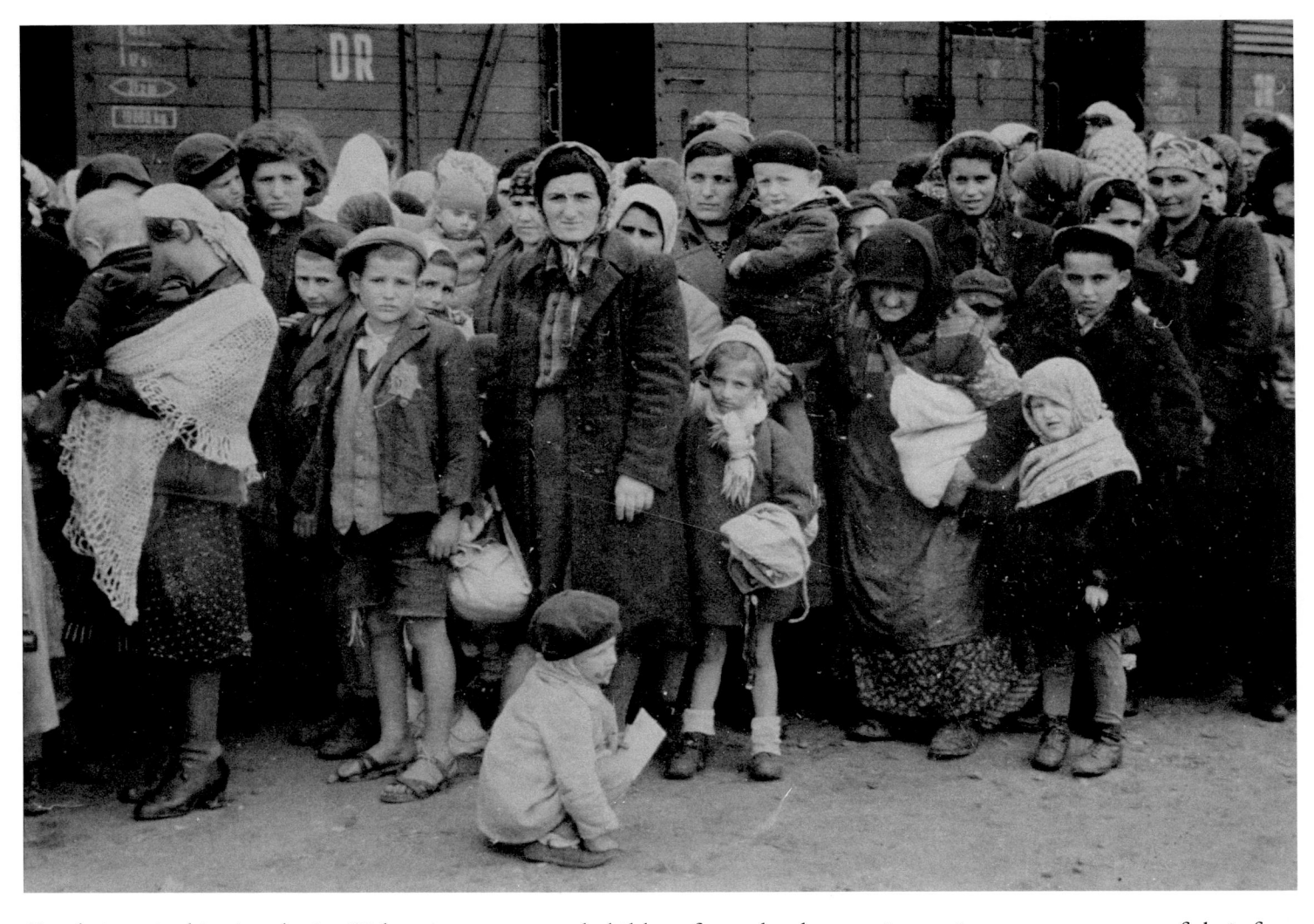

On their arrival in Auschwitz-Birkenau, women and children from the deportation trains, as yet unaware of their fate, were lined up to face a selection process. Adults considered "fit for work" were sent for slave labor. The rest – the elderly and the children – were almost always sent immediately to their deaths in the gas chambers.

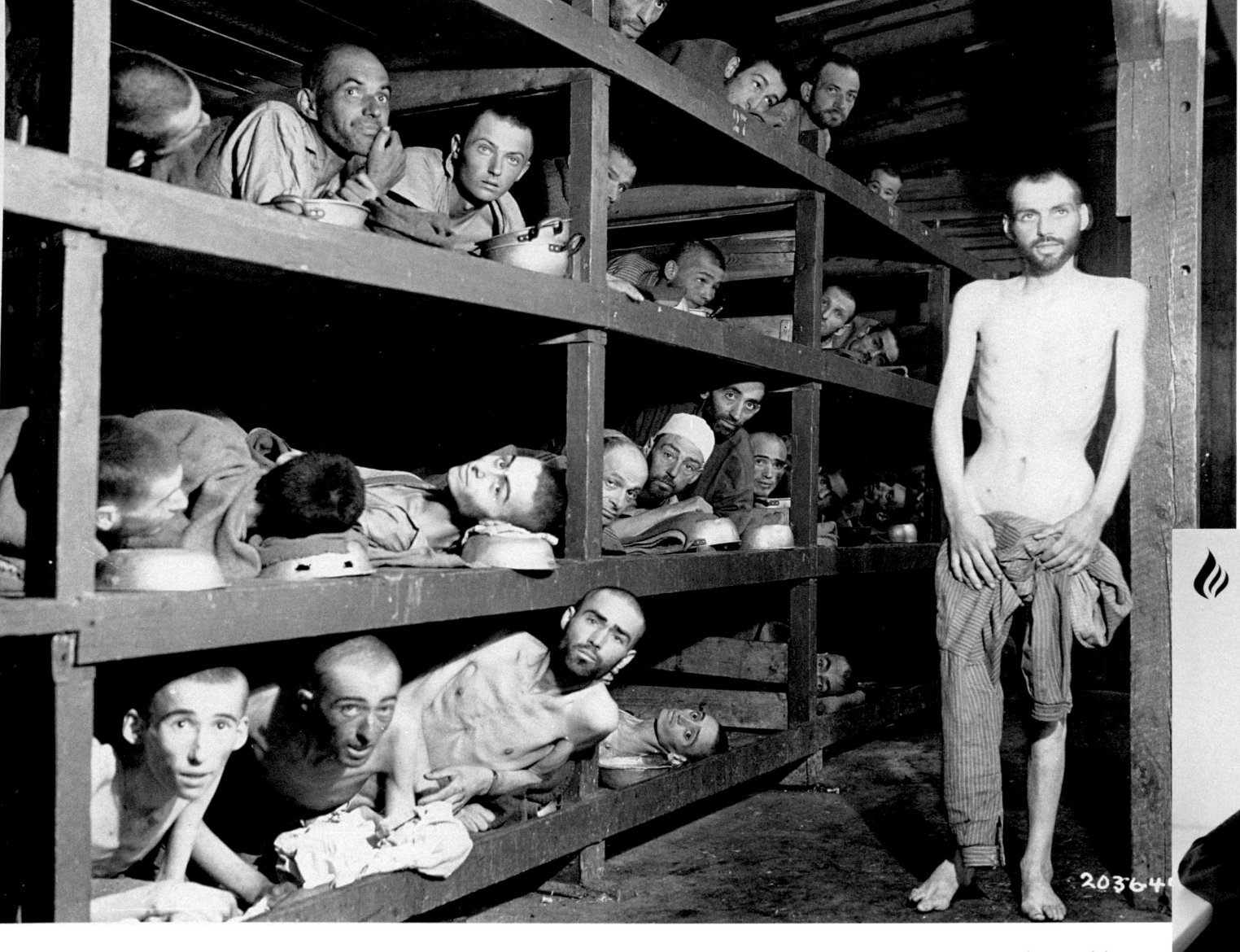

Many of the Buchenwald survivors in this photo of the camp barracks had been in other camps and endured a Death March before their liberation on April 4, 1945, by the US 89th Infantry Division. Buchenwald was the first Nazi camp liberated by US troops.

Survivor and Nobel Prize winner Elie Wiesel, right, was a Buchenwald prisoner. He's seen in the second tier from the bottom, seventh from left.

CHAPTER TWO

WHERE IT TOOK PLACE AND WHO LET IT HAPPEN

While persecution of the Jews began in 1933 in Germany with Hitler's assumption of power, the mass murder of large numbers of Jews did not begin until the onset of WWII and Nazi Germany's occupation of much of Europe.

With a few notable exceptions, the Nazis in every occupied European country, and every country controlled by Nazi-allied regimes, targeted Jews and those who assisted them – along with numerous minorities, ethnic and religious groups, and many others they deemed inferior or a threat.

The Nazis murdered their victims, the largest number of whom were Jewish, in a variety of ways. After invading Poland, many of the country's Jews were herded into ghettos where they awaited eventual transportation to slave labor or death camps. Ghettoization followed in many other countries invaded by Nazi Germany, mostly in the Soviet Union. The ghetto Jews were often rounded up and shot in random actions or died of disease or malnutrition.

From July 1941, before the death camps assumed the role for the vast majority of murders, the Nazis sent mobile killing units called *Einsatzgruppen* into various parts of eastern Europe. Together with German/Austrian SS, police, and military, as well as tens of thousands and maybe hundreds of thousands of local collaborators, by war's end they had slaughtered approximately two million Jews in town squares, forests, and pits, often burying their victims alive. In a vast array of forced labor camps – numbering some 42,500 at last count – Jews and other prisoners were often forced to work under extreme conditions; hundreds of thousands perished from arbitrary executions, disease, starvation, or from being worked to death. (According to the most recent research reported in the *New York Times*, the forms of Nazi incarceration across Europe included "30,000 slave labor camps; 1,150 Jewish ghettos; 980 concentration camps; 1,000 prisoner-of-war camps; 500 brothels filled with sex slaves; and thousands of other camps used for euthanizing the elderly and infirm, performing forced abortions, "Germanizing" prisoners or transporting victims to killing centers.")

MASS EXTERMINATION CAMPS

At the infamous Wannsee Conference held in Berlin, January 20, 1942, the Nazis formally agreed upon the establishment of a number of camps in occupied Poland whose primary purpose was mass extermination through the use of poisonous gas. The estimated numbers of murders at each camp are chilling: Auschwitz-Birkenau, 1.1 million; Treblinka, more than 870,000 (Operation Reinhard); Belzec, 500,000 (Operation Reinhard); Chelmno, 300,000; Sobibor, 250,000 (Operation Reinhard); Majdanek, 80,000. In each case, the vast majority of those sent to the gas chambers were Jewish. Jews were shipped in to the camps from every European country conquered by the Nazis or allied to them – Austria, Belgium, Bulgaria, Czechoslovakia, Denmark, Estonia, Finland, France, Germany, Greece, Hungary, Italy, Latvia, Lithuania, Luxembourg, Netherlands, Norway, Poland, Romania, Slovakia, Soviet Union (including Belarus and Ukraine), and Yugoslavia.

The Death Marches that took place toward the end of WWII forced long columns of prisoners, under heavy guard, to walk over vast distances under intolerable conditions. The marches began in the summer of 1944 and continued right up to the Third Reich's last days – the final Death March took place on May 7, the day before Germany surrendered in most places to the Allies. Approximately 750,000 prisoners, almost half of whom were Jewish, were forced on to the Death Marches and some 250,000 of those Jewish prisoners perished on the marches between the summer of 1944 and May of 1945.

Of the six million Jews who perished in the Holocaust, approximately half were murdered in the death camps, two million or more were executed by the *Einsatzgruppen* and other Nazi killing units across Europe and their collaborators, and the remaining approximately one million were killed in ghettos, slave labor camps, Death Marches, and by other methods. As was noted above, the Holocaust took place in virtually every country in Europe occupied by or allied with Nazi Germany. Notable exceptions were countries such as Albania and Denmark, where most of the Jewish population was saved through the heroic actions of local citizenry. (While Bulgaria did protect its own citizens, it deported more than 11,000 Thrace and Macedonian Jews to Treblinka, 18% of its total Jewish population.) In northern Africa, in Morocco (which was under the control of the Nazi-allied Vichy government

during much of WWII), King Mohammed V protected his Jewish citizens from deportation and certain death and refused to implement racist laws issued by the Vichy government.

Yet in far too many countries in occupied Europe, not only were the local populations indifferent to the plight of Nazi victims, but they also collaborated with Nazi Germany's murderous policies.

THE ROLE OF WEST

Just before the outbreak of WWII, an elderly Jewish man walks into a German travel agency, hoping to flee Hitler's grasp.
The travel agent hands him a globe: "Where would you like to go?" he asks him gently.
But no matter where the old man points, the travel agent says the same thing: "Sorry they don't take Jews."
Finally, in exasperation, the man looks up at the travel agent and asks: "Excuse me, maybe you have another globe?"

Tragically, while the Nazis carried on their wholesale slaughter in occupied Europe, the Western world also turned a deaf ear. The United States and Canada shut their doors tightly, not even filling the small quotas their own immigration rules had allowed for European refugees clamoring to reach their shores.

The callous indifference had begun in the pre-war period, before the wholesale slaughter of European Jews took place, which began in earnest in the summer of 1941. In June of 1939, both Canada and the United States turned away the SS *St. Louis*, which was crammed with German Jewish refugees trying to escape Hitler's viciously anti-Semitic Germany. The ship was forced to return to Europe (Britain, France, Belgium, and Holland allowed them in) where many of the passengers were subsequently murdered during the Holocaust.

Also in 1939, the United States Congress rejected the Wagner-Rogers Bill, which would have admitted 20,000 Jewish children from Germany. Laura Delano Houghteling, President Roosevelt's cousin (and wife of the US Commissioner of Immigration), noted in her opposition of the bill that "20,000 charming children would all too soon grow into 20,000 ugly adults."

Anne Frank was one of those "charming children" who could have been saved by the passage of this bill.

F.C. Blair, Canada's Minister of Immigration at the time, said that Jews trying to enter Canada reminded him of his father's farm during feeding time, with all the hogs trying to get into the trough at the same time.

After WWII ended, and the full extent of the tragedy visited upon European Jewry was known to all, a senior Canadian immigration official was asked about how many Jews would be considered for entry into Canada. His now infamous response? "None is too many."

The Holocaust that took place in Nazi-occupied Europe was, for the most part, initiated and implemented by Nazi Germany. Yet the Holocaust was also enabled by the active collaboration of local European populations and the callous indifference of Western countries.

JUST LIKE ME
Those victims of man's hatred
    were children just like me
Those who once had normal lives
    were children just like me
Those one and a half million innocent souls
    were children just like me
Yes, those children of the Holocaust
    were children just like me
And you, who killed my neighbors, my friends and my family
    You too, were children just like me
—Jody Kasner, 16, March of the Living, 1990 (excerpted)

EUROPE UNDER NAZI OCCUPATION

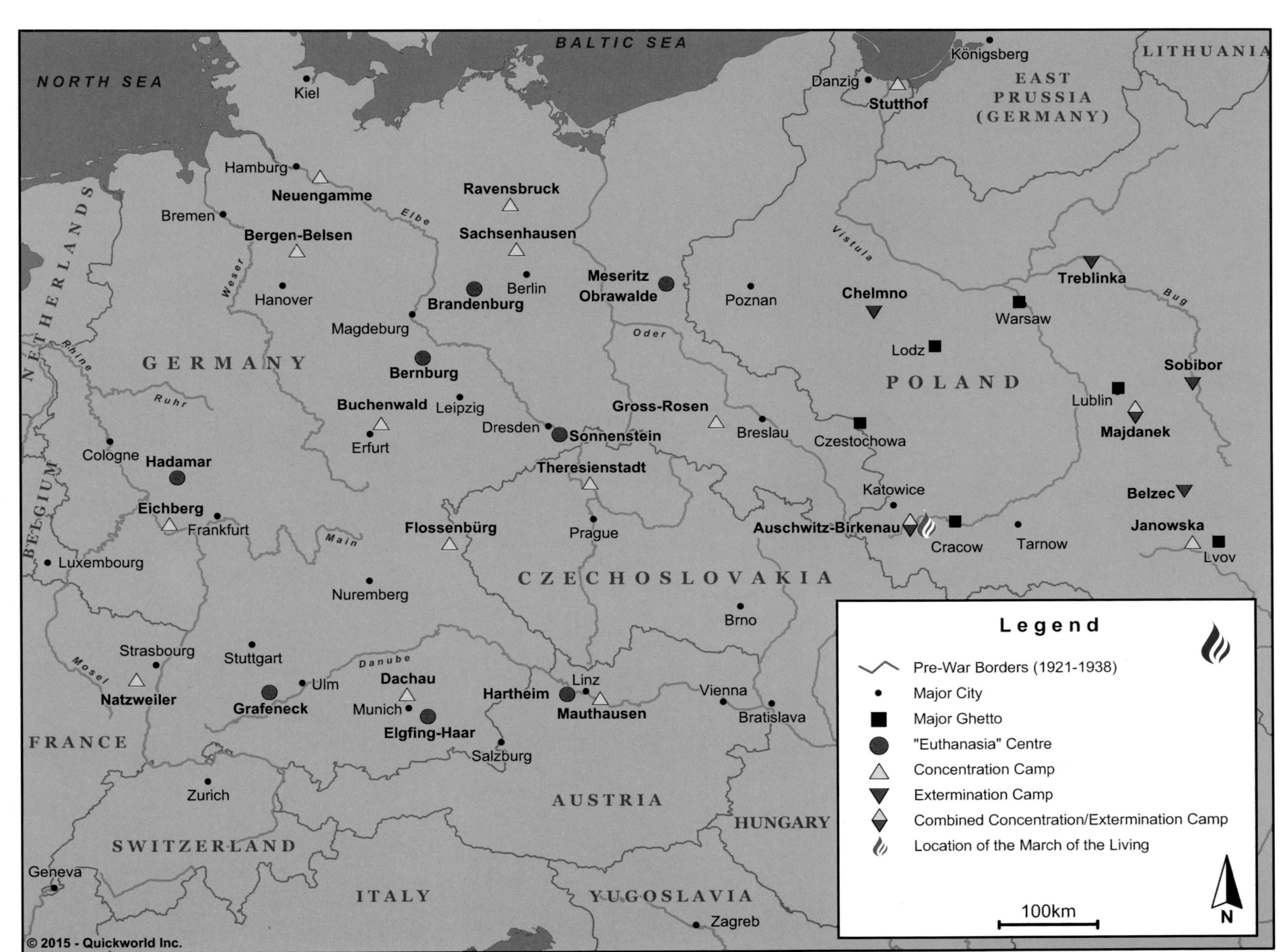

NORTH SEA

BALTIC SEA

LITHUANIA

Königsberg

EAST PRUSSIA (GERMANY)

Danzig

Kiel

Stutthof

Hamburg

Neuengamme

Ravensbruck

Bremen

Bergen-Belsen

Sachsenhausen

Treblinka

Meseritz Obrawalde

Chelmno

Hanover

Brandenburg

Berlin

Poznan

Warsaw

Bug

Magdeburg

Oder

Lodz

GERMANY

Bernburg

Sobibor

Buchenwald

Leipzig

Gross-Rosen

POLAND

Lublin

Dresden

Sonnenstein

Breslau

Majdanek

Erfurt

Czestochowa

Hadamar

Theresienstadt

Katowice

Belzec

Eichberg

Flossenbürg

Auschwitz-Birkenau

Janowska

Frankfurt

Prague

Cracow

Tarnow

Luxembourg

Lvov

Nuremberg

CZECHOSLOVAKIA

Brno

Strasbourg

Stuttgart

Danube

Linz

Vienna

Natzweiler

Grafeneck

Dachau

Hartheim

Ulm

Munich

Mauthausen

Bratislava

Elgfing-Haar

Salzburg

FRANCE

Zurich

AUSTRIA

HUNGARY

SWITZERLAND

ITALY

YUGOSLAVIA

Zagreb

Legend

⌇ Pre-War Borders (1921-1938)

• Major City

■ Major Ghetto

⬤ "Euthanasia" Centre

△ Concentration Camp

▽ Extermination Camp

◇ Combined Concentration/Extermination Camp

♨ Location of the March of the Living

100km

N

AUSCHWITZ-

The Auschwitz camp complex, built on the site of former army barracks in the Silesian district of Poland, consisted of Auschwitz I (Main Camp), Auschwitz II (Auschwitz-Birkenau), and Auschwitz III (Monowitz and the subcamps). Auschwitz I was constructed to hold Polish political prisoners, who began to arrive in May 1940. The first extermination of prisoners took place in September 1941, and Auschwitz II-Birkenau went on to become a major site of Operation Reinhard, the Nazi "Final Solution to the Jewish Question." From early 1942 until late 1944, transport trains delivered Jews from all over occupied Europe to the camp's gas chambers, where they were killed with the pesticide Zyklon B. At least 1.1 million prisoners died at Auschwitz, almost 90 percent of them Jewish; approximately one in six Jews killed in the Holocaust died at the camp. More than one-third of all Jews murdered in Auschwitz-Birkenau were of Hungarian origin – the largest of any single group. In mid-1944 and less than a year to the end of the war, within a period of only 10 weeks, approximately 400,000 Hungarian Jews were transported to Auschwitz-Birkenau, the majority of whom went directly to the gas chambers.

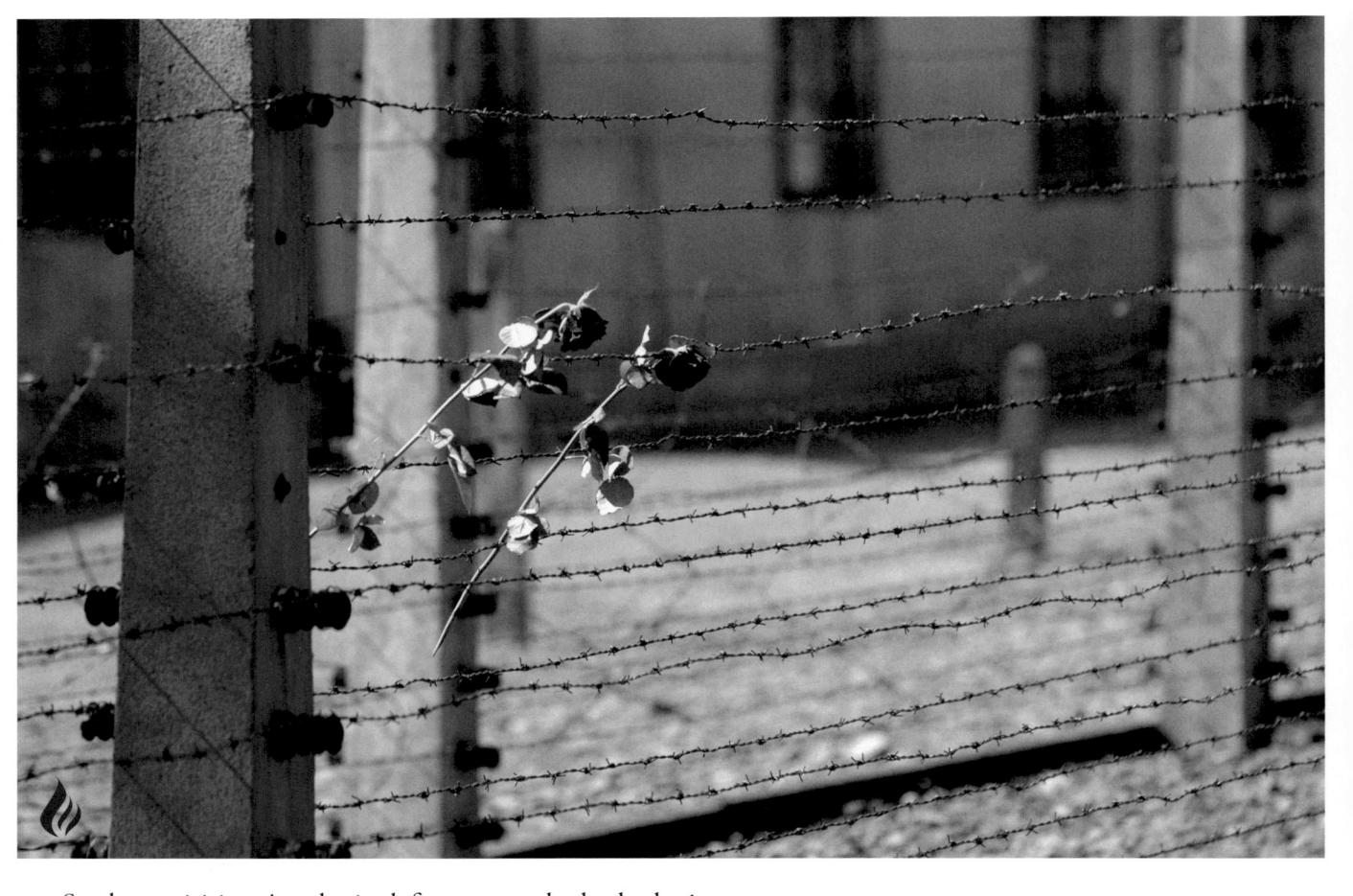

Students visiting Auschwitz left roses on the barbed wire, which was electrified to prevent prisoner escapes.

BIRKENAU

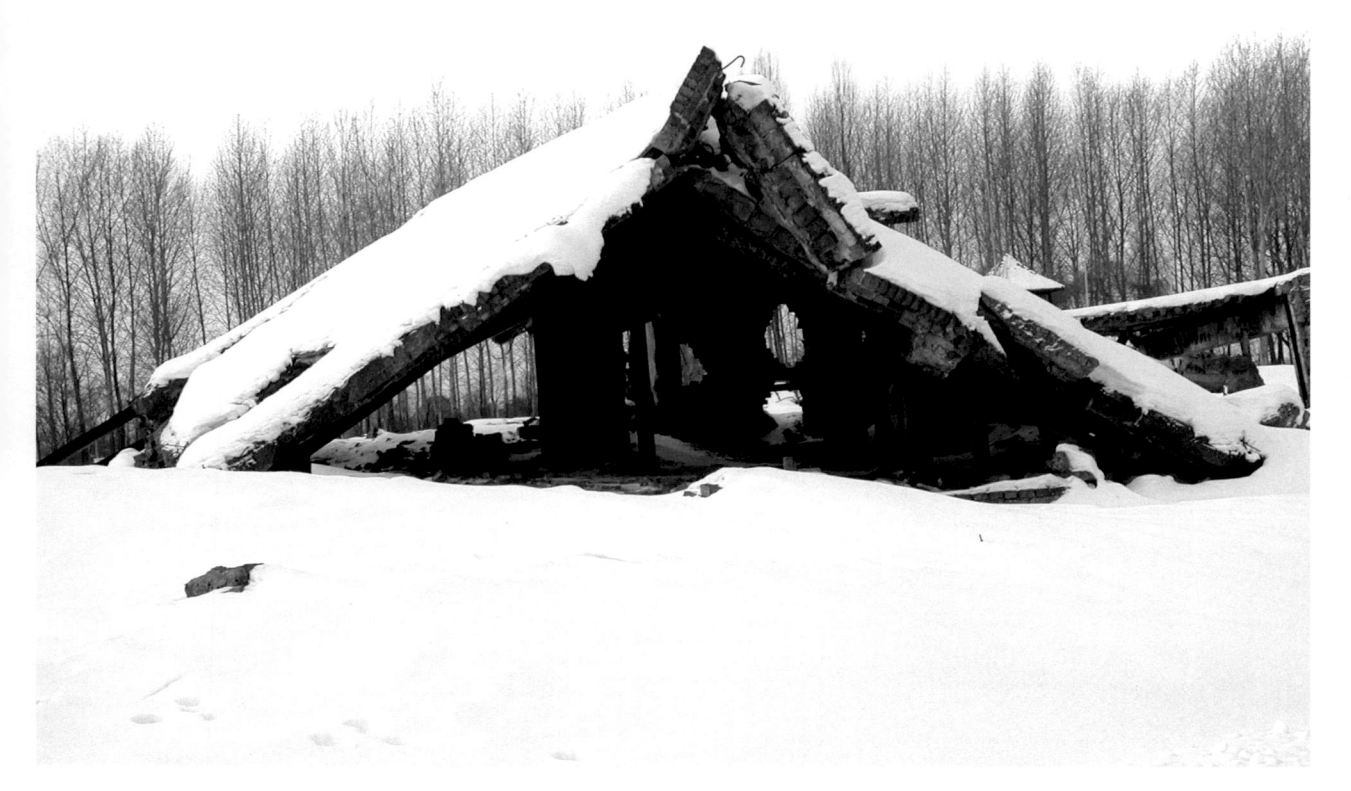

This is all that remains of Birkenau Crematorium No. 4, destroyed by Jewish *Sonderkommando* in the uprising of October 7, 1944.

In the spring of 1943, the SS completed four new crematoria in Birkenau. Although constructed to burn two corpses at once, in practice, however – according to testimony by inmates and by Auschwitz Camp Commander Rudolf Höss – this number was often exceeded. At times in the summer of 1944, during the height of the destruction of Hungarian Jews, more than 9,000 people were killed daily. At these times the incineration capacity of the ovens no longer sufficed.

The duty of the *Sonderkommando* (a special detachment of mainly Jewish prisoners) was to remove bodies from the gas chambers and operate the crematoria. Women prisoners who worked in a munitions factory smuggled gunpowder into the camp and passed it to the *Sonderkommando* for use in the uprising.

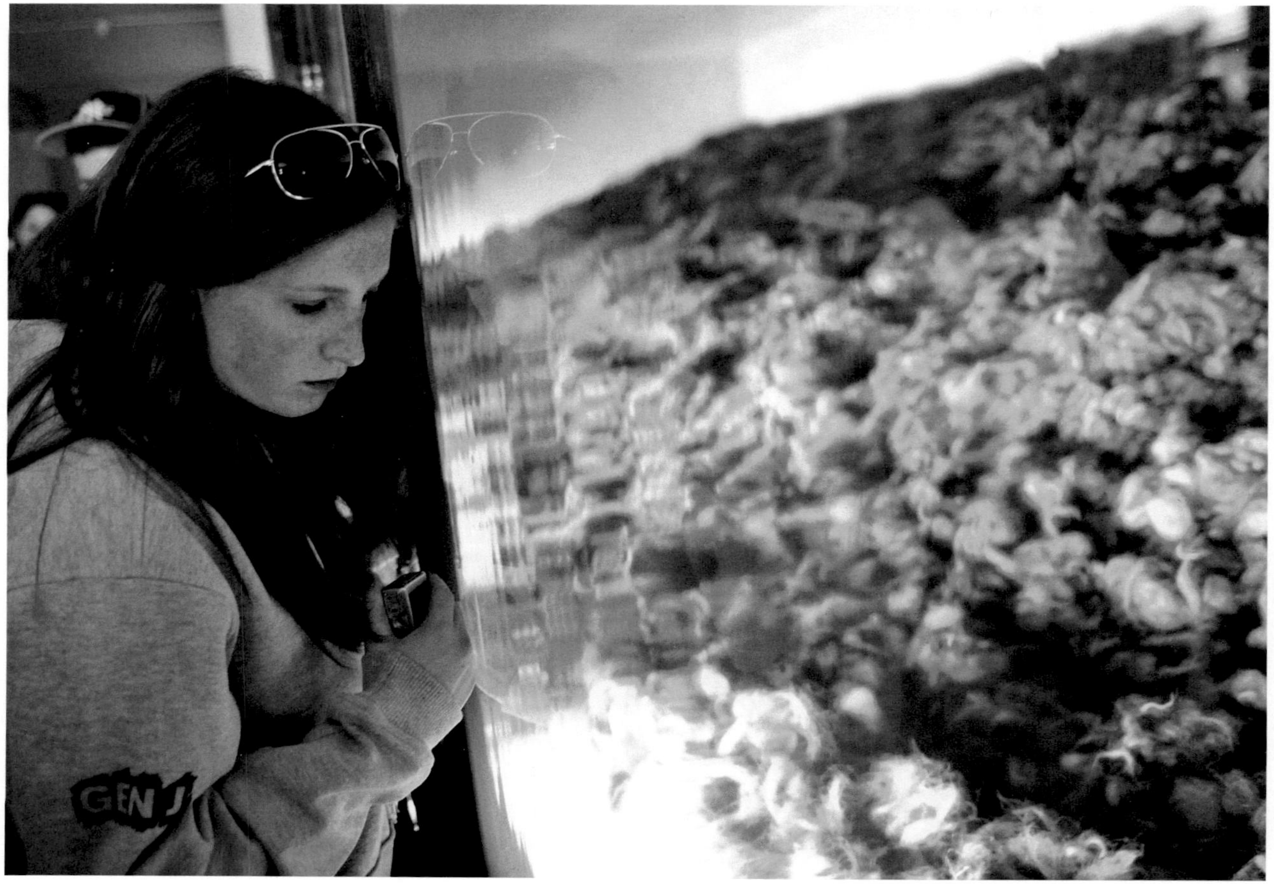

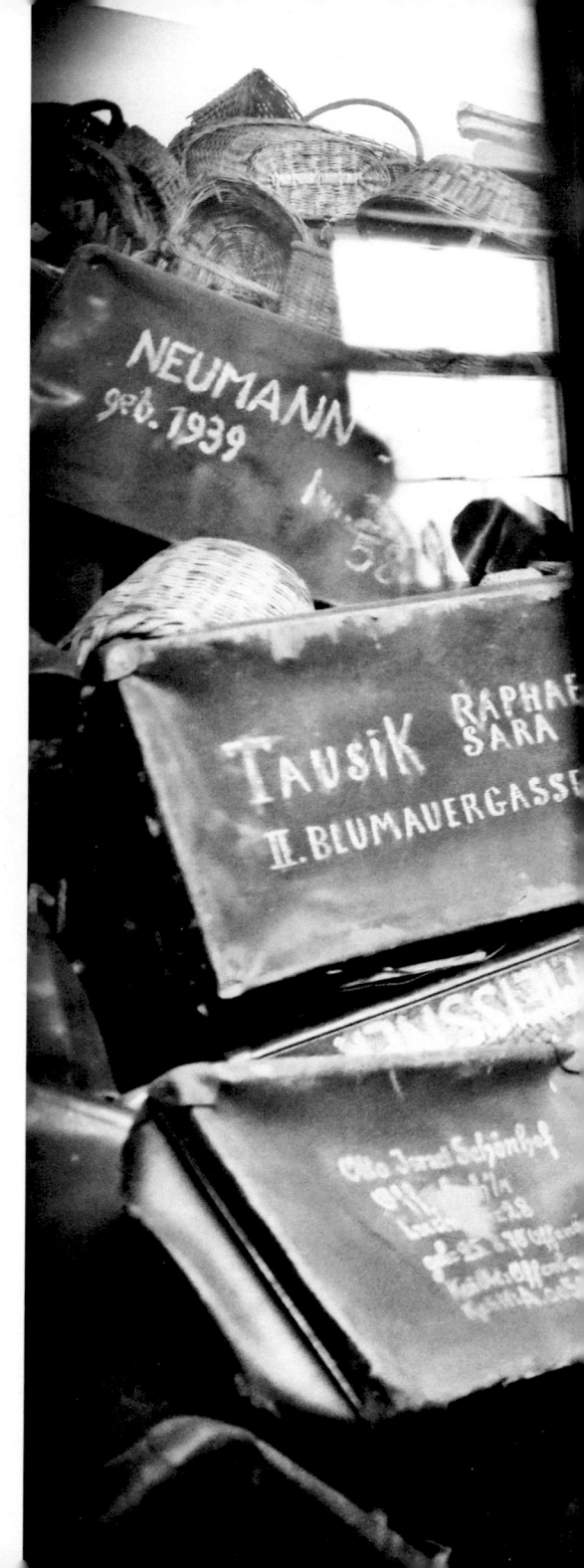

A student views the hair removed from prisoners upon their arrival at Auschwitz. Those who were not murdered immediately were issued striped uniforms, tattooed with numbers on their arms, and shaved bald in an effort to humiliate them.

The suitcases of doomed prisoners are displayed at Auschwitz. Those arriving at the camp were unaware that they would be unable to keep their personal belongings and had no idea of their ultimate fate.

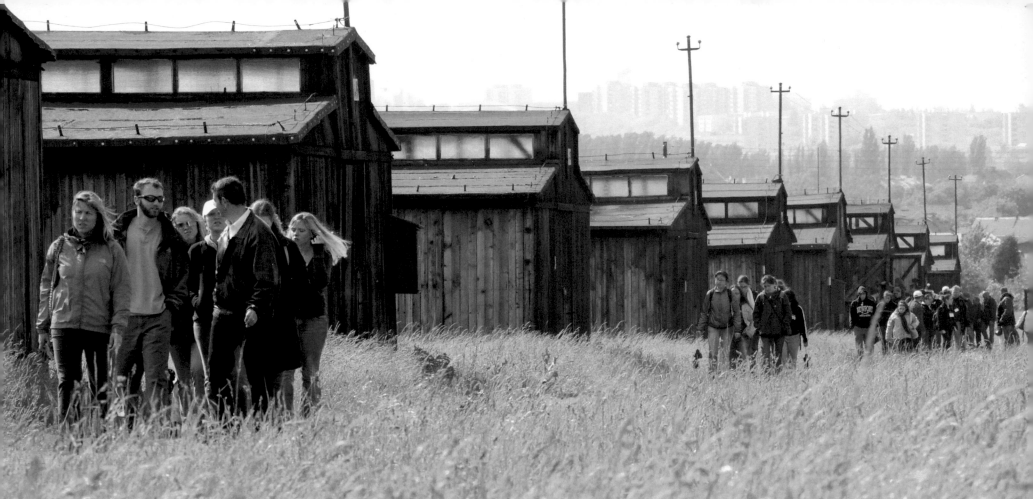

MAJDANEK

I Have Found My Parents' Grave

Anna Heilman was a survivor of the Warsaw Ghetto Uprising and the death camps of Majdanek and Auschwitz. Along with her sister, Ester Wajcblum, she helped smuggle the gunpowder into Auschwitz-Birkenau used to destroy Crematorium No. 4. Ester was executed less than two weeks before the evacuation of Auschwitz and barely three weeks before its liberation.

After her first trip back to Poland since the end of World War II, Anna wrote to the forty students who had accompanied her, saying:

"...we came to the collective grave of the ashes, a round mound of ashes that were carefully scooped to rest in one place under a protective dome of gray stone. What I felt there was relief. I have found my parents' grave. I told the students, but I suddenly felt that it was not me talking, that I was surrounded by thousands of faces, smiling at me, pushing me, talking to the students through my voice, saying: 'Tell them and thank them for coming here for remembering us and for never forgetting.'"

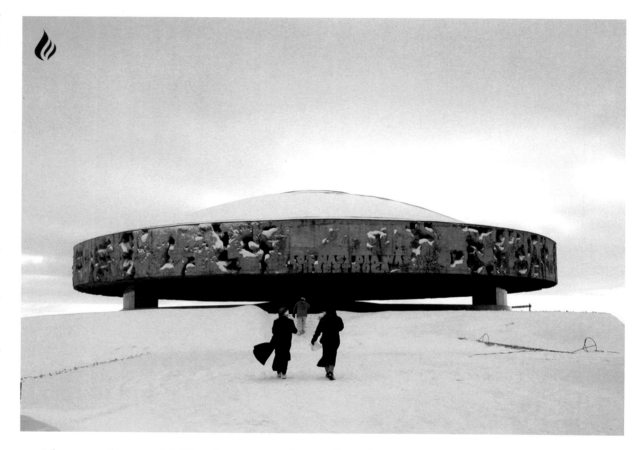

The mausoleum at Majdanek was erected in 1969 and contains ashes and remains of cremated victims that had been collected into a mound after the liberation of the camp by the Soviet Army in 1944.

26

FALLING

It is so hard to be coherent about Majdanek.
It is still all too raw for me to worry about
punctuation and sense. Some days it would
seem as if I had never gone. Others, like today, I
neglect my work to read books about the Shoah,
to go over my pictures, and to cry. It seems
that if Majdanek is real, school and society as a
whole should not be....

...what happened [during the Shoah] wasn't
okay, and there are so few words that we can
use to comfort each other. Our language rings
hollow, and when we try to form sentences,
we detract from the feeling of the shoes that
we caressed through the grates and from
the coarseness of the soil at Treblinka, as it
ran through our fingers. I have given up any
pretense of understanding. All that I know is
this: at Majdanek, I was terrified of falling into
the ashes.
—Excerpt from an essay by Lisa Gruschcow, 15

FROM ONE WHO HAS TASTED ASHES

Long I stood
staring at the mound numb
death is not a concept
not an event
it has a shape, mass, dimensions.
So I stood and stared
mouth agape
here is death
in this pile of bones and ashes.

It is cold
the wind blows
I cannot feel the cold
not on the outside
it happens
quite natural
wind, ashes
a strong gust
I squint my eyes
something in there
they start to tear

then
a taste of grit in my mouth

how can one swallow when one has
tasted ashes
how can one dare to spit them out.
—Mark Charendoff, March of the Living, 1990

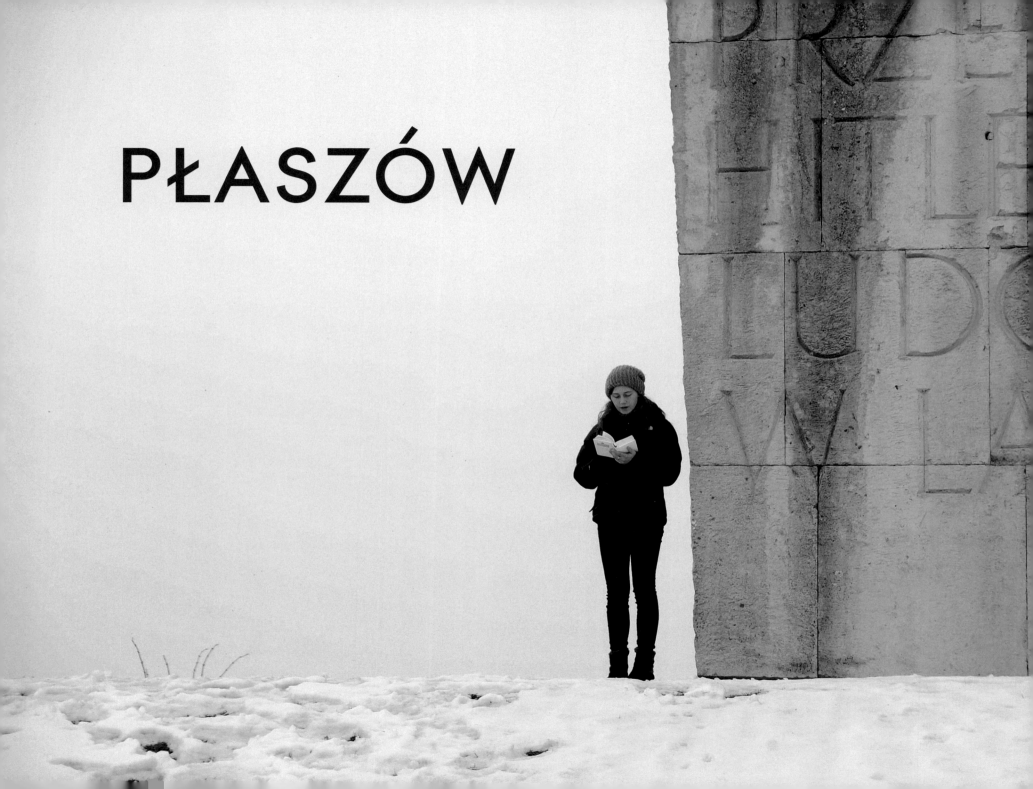

PŁASZÓW

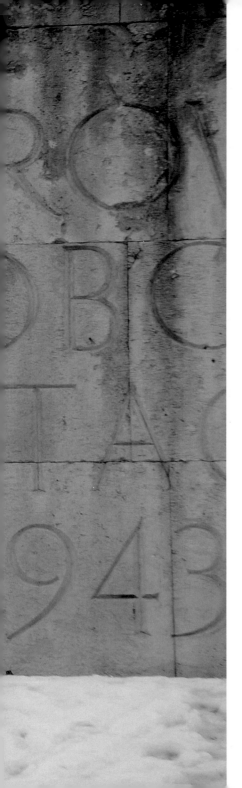

The Płaszów camp, originally intended as a forced labor camp, was constructed in a southern suburb of Kraków on the grounds of two former Jewish cemeteries in the summer of 1942, during Nazi German occupation of Poland. The deportations of the Jews from the Kraków Ghetto to Belzec began on October 28, 1942. In 1943, the camp was expanded and turned into one of many Nazi concentration camps. This monument was erected in 1964. A version of the camp is featured in Steven Spielberg's *Schindler's List*.

TREBLINKA

From July 1942 through September 1943, Treblinka operated as an extermination camp. The facility was built by Nazi Germany in occupied Poland near the village of Treblinka, northeast of Warsaw. The camp consisted of Treblinka I and Treblinka II. Treblinka I was a forced labor *Arbeitslager,* where more than half of its 20,000 inmates died from summary executions, hunger, disease, and mistreatment. Treblinka II was designed as a death factory where the Germans killed approximately 870,000 Jews, making it the deadliest of all the extermination camps in the Operation Reinhard effort.

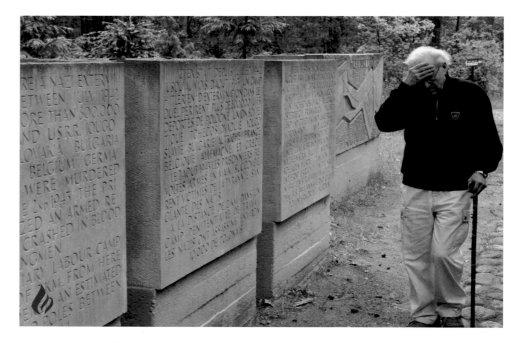

Hungarian Holocaust survivor Irving Roth enters the memorial to the victims of the Treblinka death camp located in northeastern Poland.

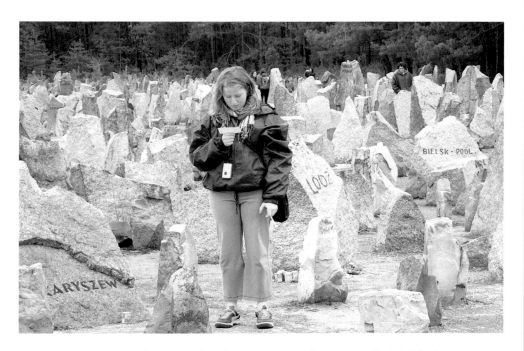

A student searches for an ancestral town at the Treblinka Memorial. The Memorial, suggestive of a cemetery, is a field of 17,000 jagged stones, 700 of which bear the names of Jewish communities in Poland obliterated during the Holocaust.

SO WRONG

I want the trees to break and fall
The grass to wither and die
I want the sky to turn black as night
The sun to go and hide
I want the air to be heavy and thick
The birds to stop singing their song
I want the stones to turn into people
To find out why humans went so wrong.
—Daniella Weber,
March of the Living, 1992

ALL AROUND ME ARE STONES

All around me are stones, but I do not feel scared; I feel comforted, assured that what I'm doing is right. It is meant to stand as a message for the world. Atrocities are atrocities, no matter how many people were involved. We have come to remember. To mark it. To show – that even though somebody – many – attempted to do us in – still we have come back. We've come back to this place to show the world that harmful things cannot go unnoticed. It has been noticed and will be marked.
—Eliyanah Delicate, 16,
March of the Living, 1990

Operation Reinhard, the code name given to the Nazi "Final Solution to the Jewish Question," was the plan to murder all Jews within their General Government territory of Poland. Operation Reinhard marked the most deadly phase of the Holocaust with the introduction of extermination camps Bełzec, Sobibór, and Treblinka. More than 1.5 million people, virtually all of whom were Jews, were murdered at these sites between December 1941 and November 1943.

Belzec, the first of the extermination camps built, was situated about a kilometer south of the local Belzec railroad station in the Lublin district of Poland, and operated from March 17, 1942, to the end of December 1942. The Nazis razed the camp in an effort to erase all evidence of the extermination center's existence. In constructing the Belzec memorial, completed in 2004, forensic scientists determined the layout of the original camp and the most appropriate layout for a memorial. The pathway shown at right is thought to be the original camp road, since it was the only earth devoid of human remains.

BELZEC

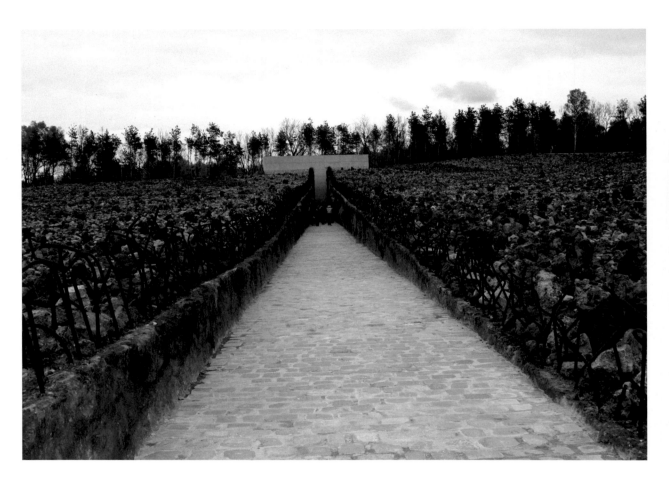

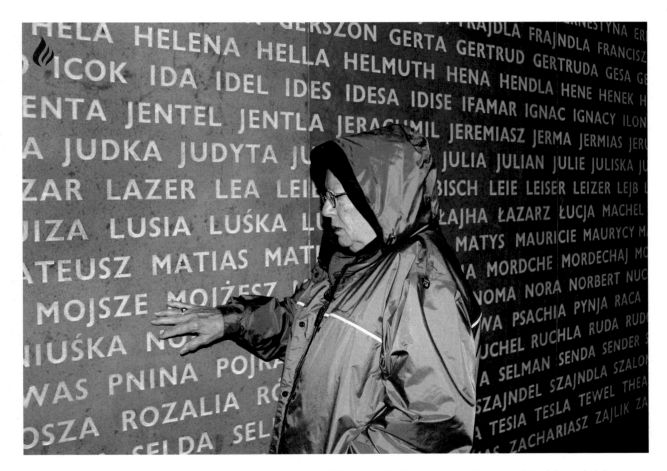

Anita Ekstein, Holocaust survivor and hidden child, visited the Belzec death camp memorial where her mother, Ettel, was murdered. The names of the camp's victims are inscribed on the memorial wall.

I Miss My Mommy and My Little Brother

"In the Holocaust archives, there is a letter written in 1943 by a Jewish girl by the name of Deborah Katz. She was nine years old when she and her family were loaded into cattle trains destined for the death camp of Belzec. Her parents managed to pry open a window of the car and threw the child out hoping that a miracle would happen and she would be saved. A Catholic nun happened to pass by and found the injured child. She took her to the convent, hid her among the sisters, and nursed her back to health. The child was in comparative safety and she had a good chance to survive. One morning, the nuns woke up and found a letter on Deborah's bed. This is what the child wrote: *It's bright daylight but there is darkness around me. The sun is shining, but there is no warmth coming from it. I miss my Mommy and my little brother, Moses, who always played with me. I can't stand being without them any longer and I want to go where they are.* The following morning, Deborah Katz was put by the Gestapo on the next trainload. Destination: the gas chambers of Belzec."

—Miles Lerman, Survivor
Opening of Belzec Memorial, June 3, 2004

CHAPTER THREE

WHO RESISTED? AND HOW?

The horror and scale of the atrocities that took place during WWII often mask another aspect of this history: the heroic resistance that so many showed in the face of unimaginable cruelty.

During the students' encounter with the Holocaust in Europe, they hear the stories of resistance and meet with some of those who risked their lives to save Jews, and, when possible, with WWII veterans who liberated the camps where the Nazis imprisoned the survivors.

Why must this other side be told? So that the entire picture of the Holocaust is shown. So that the study of the Holocaust does not cause us to give up completely on humanity. So that these courageous people who resisted can serve as role models in our own lives.

Spiritual resistance throughout the war was shown by millions of the Nazis' victims who displayed remarkable courage in adhering to their faith and values. From Jehovah's Witnesses, who refused to join Hitler's war, courageous church leaders, such as Dietrich Bonhoffer, who spoke out against Nazi policies at the cost of their own lives, to Hitler's Jewish victims, who maintained their faith and dignity even during the most difficult of times – all refused to let their spirits be crushed in the face of overwhelming brutality. Young girls and women, like Jewish Anne Frank in the Netherlands and Christian Krystyna Wituska in Poland, wrote words in hiding and in prison that reflected an unbroken spirit and a moral conviction and love for humanity that has outlived the hate-filled Nazi proclamations. The Polish Jewish doctor Janusz Korczak refused to abandon his 200 young orphans even after numerous offers of help from Polish friends outside the Warsaw Ghetto. Instead, when the Nazi deportation order arrived, he led a march through the streets of Warsaw with his orphans – clutching their favorite toys and their handmade flags – to the waiting train that took them to Treblinka, where they met their fate with 870,000 other Jews. "The very stones of the street," wrote Yiddish novelist Yehoshua Perle, "wept at the sight of the procession."

Physical resistance came from both partisans and liberators. In fact, there were large numbers of armed uprisings against the Nazis throughout Europe. Most had little chance of success, given the overwhelming military might and brutality of the Nazi enemy.

On April 19, 1943, the remaining Jews trapped in the Warsaw Ghetto launched the heroic Warsaw Ghetto Uprising. The Germans had planned to liquidate the Warsaw ghetto in three days, but the stubborn ghetto fighters held out for four weeks. Thirteen thousand Jews were killed in the ghetto during the uprising – many of whom were burnt alive.

The Warsaw Uprising, which began in August of 1944, was the largest single military revolt initiated by European resistance fighters during World War II. The courageous Polish resistance – led by the *Armia Krajowa* (Polish Home Army) – fought for sixty-three days, with almost no outside assistance, until they were crushed by the Nazis. In addition to thousands of military casualties, some 200,000 Polish civilians died, the majority during mass executions, and some 250,000 were exiled from the city. By the end of the war, more than three-quarters of the city had been destroyed.

Throughout Europe, Jewish partisan and resistance units displayed remarkable courage in resisting the enemy in the face of the overwhelming military superiority of the Nazi war machine. An estimated 30,000 Jewish men and women served as partisans in the forests in Poland alone. Armed Jewish resistance took place in approximately sixty ghettos, three major concentration/death camps, and eighteen forced labor camps.

From outside occupied Europe, the Allied armies fought to liberate Europe from the deathly grip of Nazi Germany. In the latter stages of the war, with the Soviets approaching from the east, and the other Allied forces from the west and south, Nazi Germany's hold over Europe began to crumble.

When these forces encountered the labor camps and death camps, they came across thousands upon thousands of corpses and emaciated prisoners who seemed more dead than alive. Indeed, many perished in the immediate days following their liberation as a result of the years of torture and deprivation they endured.*

Those who did survive lived the rest of their days with a feeling of deep gratitude for those who liberated them – at the last moment – from the jaws of death, often referring to them as "angels" in their post-Holocaust memoirs.

---

* For the sake of historical accuracy, of course, one must distinguish between the various forms of physical resistance. The national movements, such as the Polish Home Army (often rife with anti-Semitism), had a different motivation from the Jews in their fight against the Nazis, just as the Allies did. Their impetus was not to save European Jewry, but to defeat Hitler. Further, uprisings by Jews against overwhelming odds and abandoned by the entire world, are not comparable to organized armies fighting with the support of their governments and fellow citizens.

As well, individuals who are now called Righteous Among the Nations risked their lives during the Holocaust to save Jews from murder at the hands of the Nazis. Today, more than 25,000 names of the women and men who have been given this honorific title by the State of Israel appear in Yad Vashem, Israel's national Holocaust Museum. The rescuers hailed from every country in Europe and from every possible background. They were young and old, Christian, Muslim, believers, atheists, society's aristocrats, and humble peasant farmers. All of them risked life and limb, sometimes for years, to save thousands of Jews who were often complete and utter strangers.

These are people such as Swedish diplomat Raoul Wallenberg – who along with other diplomats such as Charles Lutz, Fredrich Born, Angela Rota, and Georgia Perlasca – saved tens of thousands of Hungarian Jews and then disappeared into the Soviet Gulag; the German factory owner Oskar Schindler, who boldly rescued more than 1,000 Jews destined for the death camps; and the Polish nurse and underground worker Irena Sendler who, together with fellow Polish underground members, smuggled Jewish children out of the Warsaw Ghetto to live in monasteries and with Polish families under assumed identities. "I was brought up to believe that a person must be rescued when drowning, regardless of religion and nationality," Sendler said. (Sendler was part of *Zegota*, the Polish Council to Aid Jews, an underground resistance effort that helped thousands to find places of safety in occupied Poland.)

The Righteous Among the Nations displayed courage, bravery, and altruism beyond belief. They took enormous risks, and even sacrificed their lives, to save others. It has been aptly stated that the Righteous Among the Nations did not only save Jews during the Holocaust, they also saved the very reputation of humanity.

Dr. Naomi Azrieli reminds us that we must remember this part of the Holocaust story as well. "No one survived the Holocaust without the help of another." It could have been a hiding place, an extra ration, a pair of shoes – even a kind gesture. It is these acts of nobility we must remember, along with the all too familiar acts of Nazi horror and cruelty and the willing participation of their collaborators. Our young people must be given hope for the future and an understanding that evil was indeed resisted during the darkest of times – and can still be confronted today.

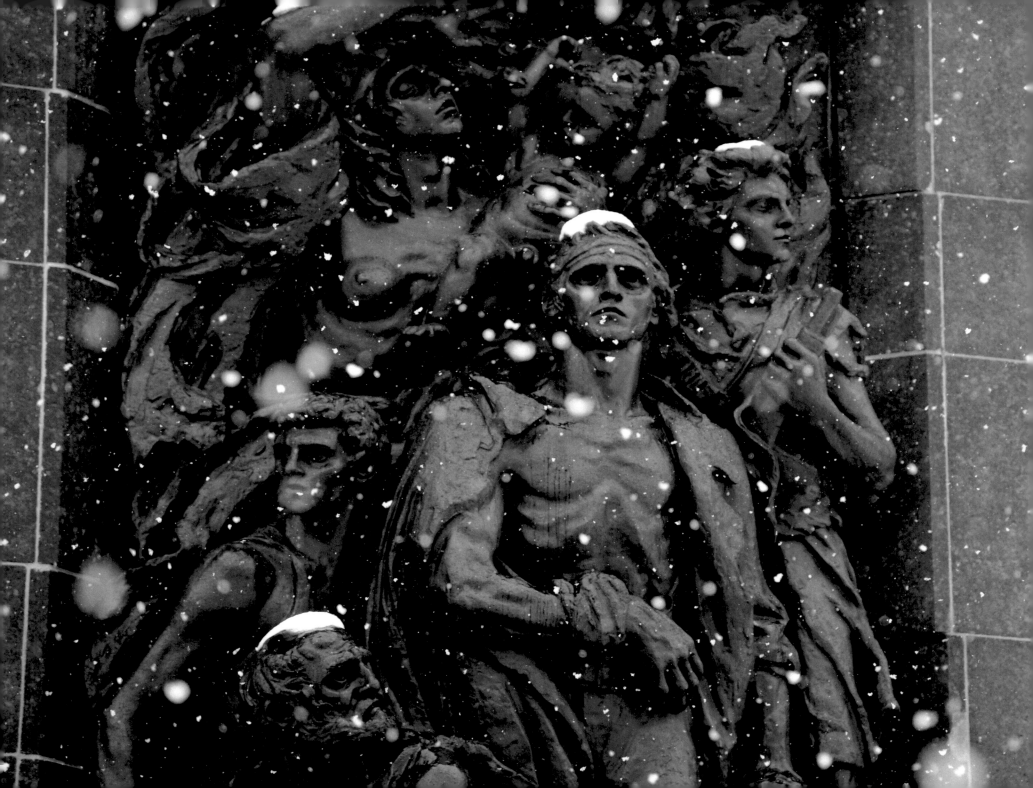

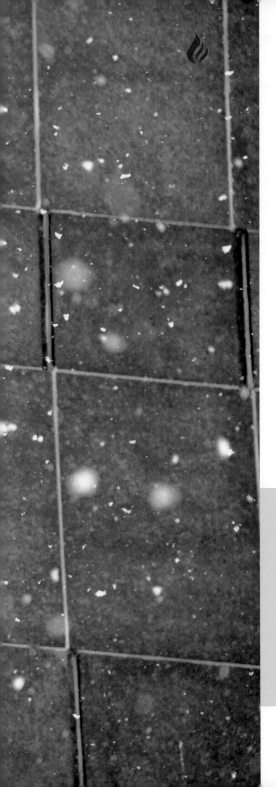

TO EACH OF THEM

And to each of them, I will give a name
and a monument
To every man, to every woman, to
every child
And to each of them, I will give a name
and a monument
To those who fought
And to those who had no way to fight
To those who sang on their way to
their deaths
And to those who were silent
To those who found God in the camps
And to those who declared God dead
And to each of them, I will give a name
and a monument

To those who went hungry so their
children could eat
And to those who stole their children's
bread in the night
To those who displayed the strength of
the human spirit
And to those who let the pain overtake
them
And to each of them, I will give a name
and a monument
To those who were there
When every bite of bread was a decision
When every step could cause death
To the heroes and to the non-heroes
The strong and the weak
To those who were superhuman
And to those who, like you and I
Were merely, most importantly
Human
—Aviva Goldberg, 17,
March of the Living, 1990

On April 19, 1943 a small band of Jewish fighters launched the heroic Warsaw Ghetto Uprising, holding off the mighty German army for almost a month. Ultimately, the Nazis defeated them, but only after burning down the entire ghetto. The Rapoport Memorial in Warsaw features sculpted images of the ghetto fighters, led by Mordechai Anielewicz, who fell during the uprising.

RESISTANCE THROUGH

KRYSTYNA WITUSKA (1920–1944)
A Young Polish Heroine

I am First a Human Being

Krystyna Wituska was born near Lodz, Poland, in 1920. After the Nazis evicted her family from their home she came to Warsaw with her mother and saw firsthand the brutal treatment of its Jewish population. She later fell in love with Karol Szapira, a Jewish boy hiding in Warsaw. In 1941 she joined the Polish underground but was arrested in 1942 and sent to the Alt-Moabit Prison in Berlin. She continued to write from prison to her family and to Karol, who was shot by the Nazis in 1943, a fact her family kept from her. Krystyna Wituska was beheaded on June 26, 1944 in Halle-Saale, near Leipzig. Today, a monument in her memory stands in Halle-Saale, initiated by Irmgard Sinner, the daughter of Werner Lueben, the officer who sentenced Wituska to death.

"On the day that I die I want to die for freedom and justice and for all humanity and not just for my Poland. I am first a human being and then a Pole…. Consciousness of a universal humanity will comfort me. But please don't misunderstand. It is not that I don't love my country, but I would relinquish my country's objectives, if they were not also good for all of humanity."

"If you have a good understanding of life, you know how to accept death. The important thing is to maintain one's human dignity to the end."

ANNE FRANK (1929–1945)

I Still Believe that People are Good at Heart

Anne Frank, perhaps the most well-known victim of the Holocaust, was a talented and sensitive writer. She and her family were hidden by their Dutch friends, until they were betrayed and sent to Auschwitz-Birkenau. Her entire family, with the exception of her father, perished in the Holocaust. Anne died in Bergen-Belsen in March of 1945, just a few months before the war's end, at the young age of 15. Her diary, later called The Diary of a Young Girl, *was published after the war and has sold millions of copies and been translated into many languages.*

"How wonderful it is that nobody need wait a single moment before starting to improve the world."

"It's really a wonder that I haven't dropped all my ideals, because they seem so absurd and impossible to carry out. Yet I keep them, because in spite of everything, I still believe that people are really good at heart."

"No one has ever become poor by giving."

"I hear the approaching thunder that, one day, will destroy us too, I feel the suffering of millions. And yet, when I look up at the sky, I somehow feel that this cruelty too shall end, and that peace and tranquility will return once again."

WRITING

HANNAH SENESH (1921–1944)

Blessed is the Heart with the Strength to Stop Beating for Honor's Sake

The poet Hannah Senesh emigrated from Hungary to Palestine in 1939 after experiencing anti-Semitism as a child in her native country. She lived on a kibbutz on the seashore near Caesarea. When World War II broke out, she and other Jewish residents of Palestine volunteered to fight the Nazis. She was trained by the British as a paratrooper, and was dropped behind Nazi lines in Europe. The Nazis captured, tortured, and executed the 23-year-old on November 7, 1944. She left us a remarkable legacy of poetry.

Stars

There are stars whose radiance is visible on earth though they have long disappeared.
There are people whose brilliance continues to light the world though they are no
longer among the living. These lights are particularly bright when the night is dark.
They light the way for humanity.

Blessed is the Match

Blessed is the match consumed in kindling the flame
Blessed is the flame that burns in the secret fastness of the heart
Blessed is the heart with the strength to stop beating for honor's sake
Blessed is the match consumed in kindling the flame

Oh Lord, My God—

Oh Lord, my God,
I pray that these things never end:
The sand and the sea,
The rush of the waters,
The crash of the heavens,
The prayer of the heart.

41

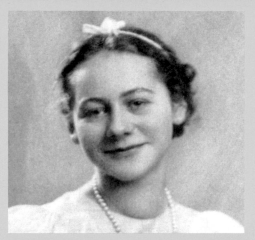

Krystyna Wituska

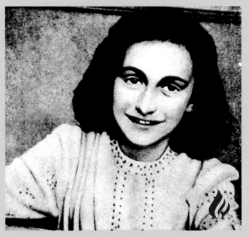

Anne Frank

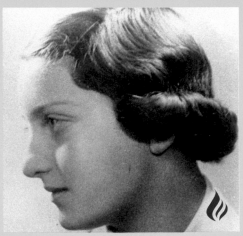

Hannah Senesh

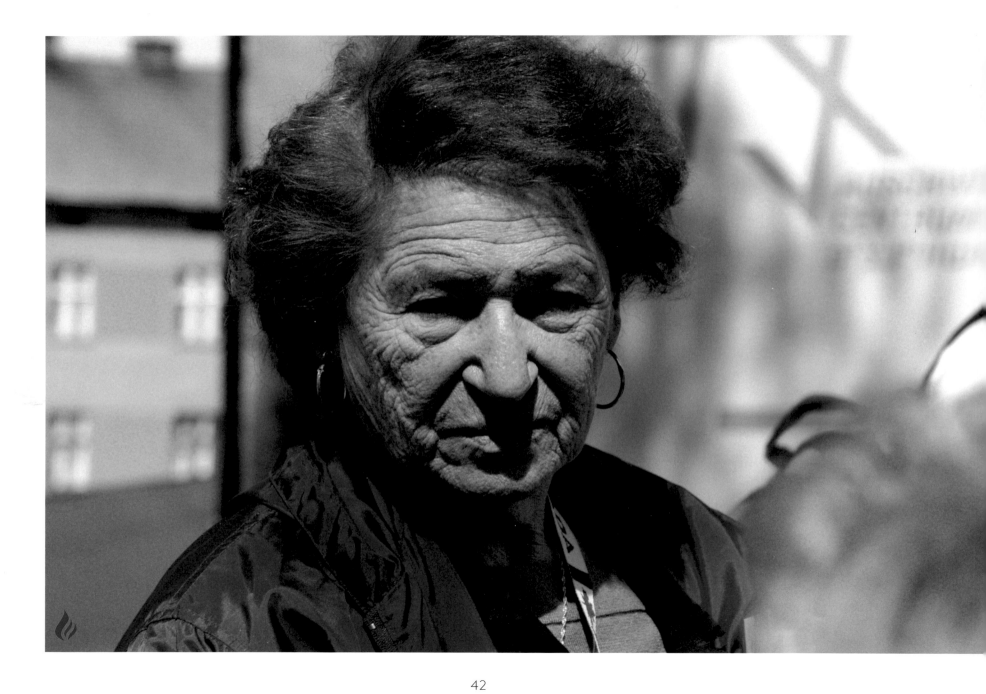

So The World Does Not Forget

Bronka Krygier, a Jewish Partisan during the Holocaust, traveled with students on several March of the Living trips before her death in 2010. After the 2004 March of the Living, she said:

> *"To see the [death camps], to touch them, reminds me of the tragedy of my people and the Six Million who should not have died, who should not have been murdered. Those we must remember…the children must be witness to the truth of this past. The tragic lessons and legacy must be passed on to the children so they can be watchful, so they can be certain the world does not forget."*

Bronka was caught several times by the Nazis. On one occasion, she was lined up in front of a firing squad, but was freed by a group of partisans at the last moment. On another occasion, she was accused by a Polish boy of being a Jew. But Bronka kept arguing she was Polish, and the Nazis themselves were not certain. At one point in the interrogation, which was conducted in German, then translated into Polish, the Nazi officer said, "*Nu Chana retz neisht kayn Yiddish?*" (So Chana do you not speak any Yiddish at all?) Bronka almost fell for the trap, but at the last moment, she held herself back and said in Polish, "Please translate."

At that point one of the Nazis said, "She might not be Jewish, but just look at her nose…"

Bronka stared back, and then pointed to the Nazi officer's nose, which apparently was just as big as hers, and said, "And him? What about his nose?"

Bronka's quick retort may have saved her life, but not some of her teeth. The enraged officer took his gun and smacked Bronka across the face, knocking out several of her teeth.

"A hundred children, a hundred individuals who are people – not people-to-be, not people of tomorrow, but people now, right now – today."

Janusz Korczak, until the last moment of his life, dedicated himself to the rights of children. He was one of the first people in history to understand that children were not potential people, not half-adults, but individuals who deserved full respect and dignity each and every day of their lives. Korczak ran orphanages in Warsaw before and during the war, wrote children's stories, was on Polish radio, and, even today, is a beloved figure in the eyes of many Poles.

Dr. Korczak had one rule that he almost never broke – never lie to children – a rule he was forced to violate one tragic day in August of 1942, when the Nazis ordered him and his children to report to the train station for their deportation to Treblinka death camp. Giving up a number of last-minute chances of escape for himself, Korczak asked the children to prepare for a picnic. They got dressed, grabbed their favorite dolls and other objects, and off they marched through the streets of Warsaw to the cattle cars, in which they were transported to Treblinka and murdered together with some 870,000 souls, almost all Jews.

Today, there are 17,000 jagged stones and markers in Treblinka, many with the names of the Jewish communities destroyed in the Holocaust, but only one stone bears the name of a single person – Dr. Janusz Korczak.

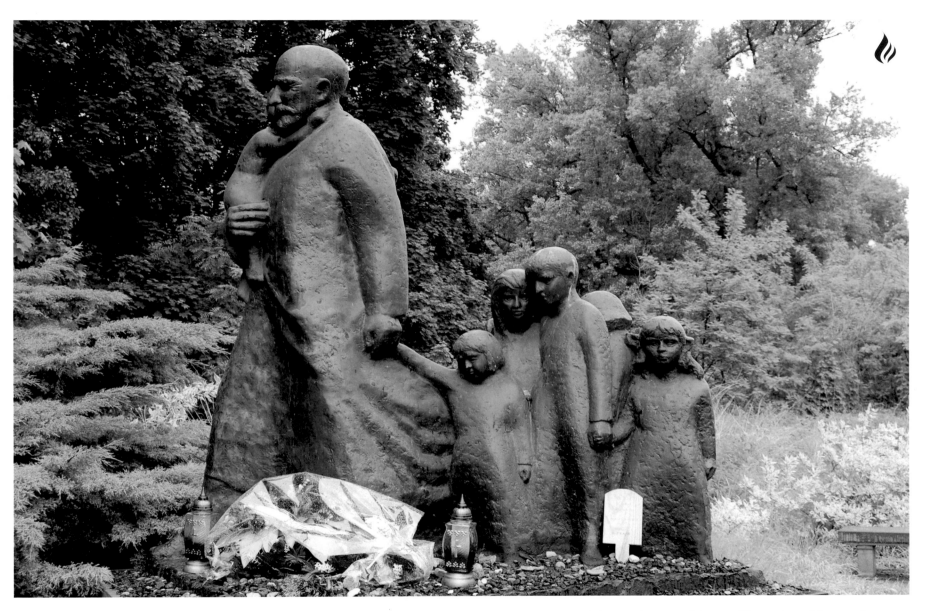

This sculpture of Janusz Korczak and his orphans on their way to deportation to Treblinka stands as a tribute in Warsaw's Jewish Cemetery.

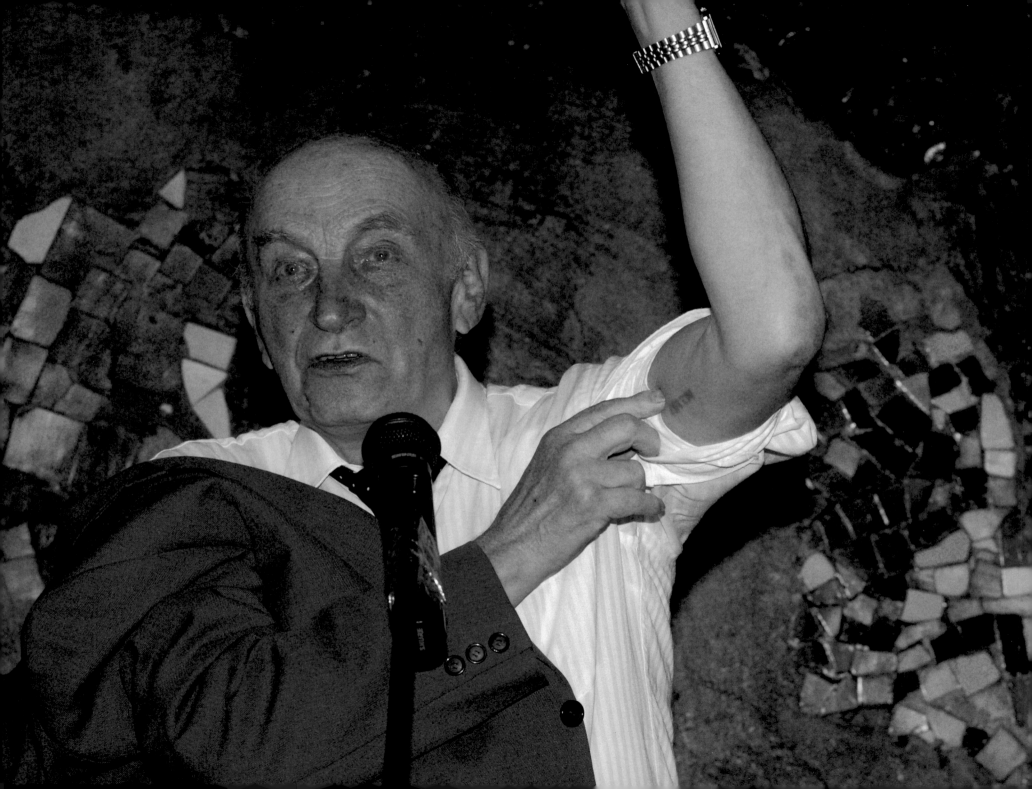

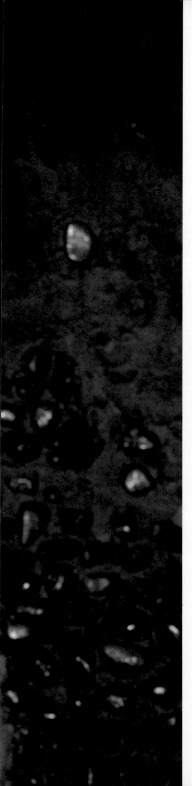

Jerzy Kozminski – Righteous Among the Nations

Righteous Among the Nations is an honorific title conferred on those who risked their lives during the Holocaust to save Jews from extermination by the Nazis. At the age of 17, Jerzy Kozminski (1924-2010) and his mother Renia smuggled out all 13 members of the Glazer family, one by one in a horse and buggy on the night of the Warsaw Ghetto Uprising. The Kozminskis hid the Glazers in the basement of their home on the outskirts of Warsaw for more than a year. Jerzy, a member of the Polish underground, was captured and tortured by the Nazis, but did not disclose that 13 Jews were hiding in his family's basement. Jerzy was deported to Auschwitz and then to Mauthausen, where he was liberated by American troops in May of 1945.

Over the years, many Righteous Among the Nations have participated in the March of the Living and shared their stories with the students as did Jerzy Kozminski. Christian, Muslim, agnostic, and atheist, from almost every nation in Europe – 25,000 have been recognized as Righteous.

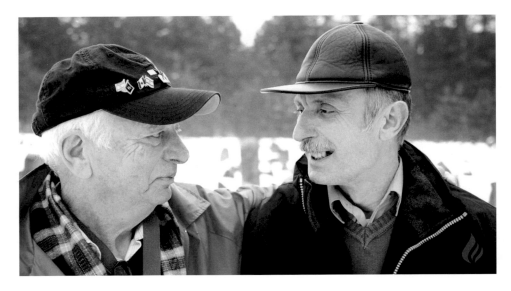

Righteous Reunion

Sidney Zoltak grew up in the village of Siemiatycze in eastern Poland. During the Holocaust, at the age of 11, he escaped to live in the forest. He was eventually sheltered in a barn for 14 months by the Krynski family.

In 2014, he returned to his hometown to reunite with remaining members of the Krynski family. In his story, told in the presence of the son of his rescuer and recorded at Treblinka, where nearly one million Jews were murdered, he relates that of all of his classmates, he is the only one who survived.

"When we got back to our hometown, less than one percent had survived. Less than 70 from a community of 7,000. The most difficult part for me was that none of my classmates, none of my friends survived. I am the only one. I think about it. The only reunion I can have is in this place among the memorial stones…" Then turning to Stanislaw Krynski, the son of his rescuer, he said, "I feel like kissing him."

Righteous Among the Nations Zygmunt Krynski (right), kissing his friend Sidney Zoltak, in front of the barn where he hid Sidney during the war.

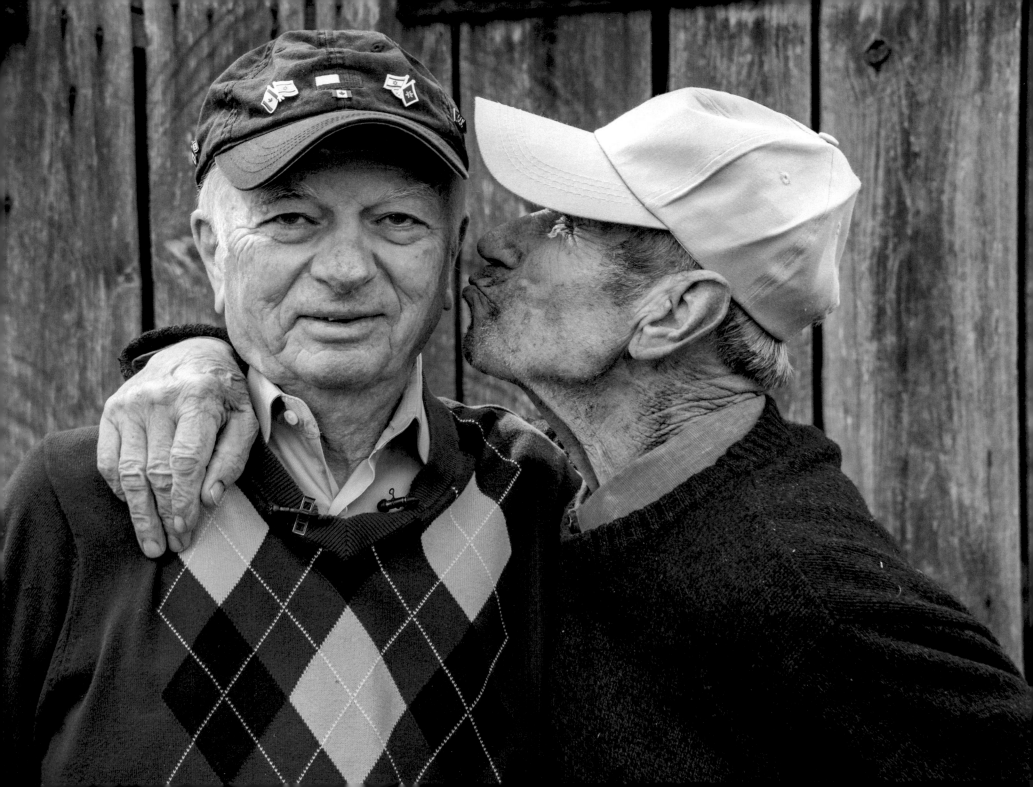

What We Have Is What We Give

Born in Grodno, Poland, Felix Zandman survived the Holocaust with the help of a courageous family of Catholic Polish Righteous Among the Nations. Jan and Anna Puchalski hid him and his uncle for 17 months. (Anna, the family's housekeeper, remembered the kindness Felix's grandmother had shown her in times of trouble.) Their main hiding place was a dugout 170 cm long, 150 cm wide and 120 cm tall that they shared with two other Jewish escapees. His uncle, Sender Freydowicz, taught Felix trigonometry and advanced mathematics in the long hours of darkness. After the war, Felix went on to become a scientist, inventor, and philanthropist, founding an electronics company employing more than 22,000 people worldwide. His inventions continue to be used today.

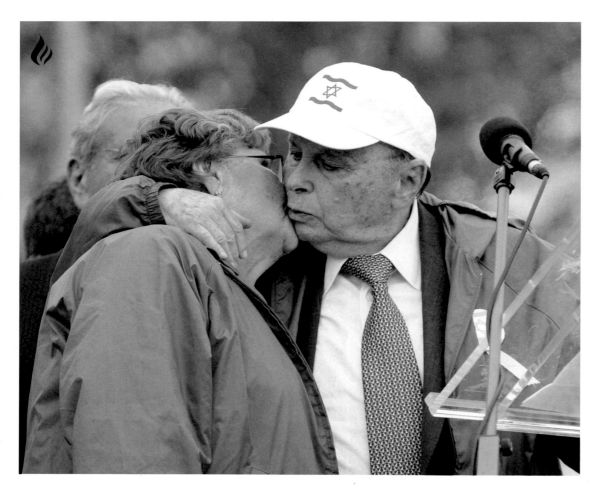

The late Felix Zandman kisses in gratitude one of his rescuers, Krystyna Puchalski-Maciejewskai, as he shares his story with thousands of March of the Living students during the 2008 program in Auschwitz-Birkenau. Krystyna, along with her two siblings and parents, are honored as Righteous Among the Nations. Zandman's inspiration was his grandmother who taught him:

"What we have is what we give.
If you give to somebody,
you give yourself.
Nobody can take it away from
you, even after your death.
If you give, this stays with you forever."

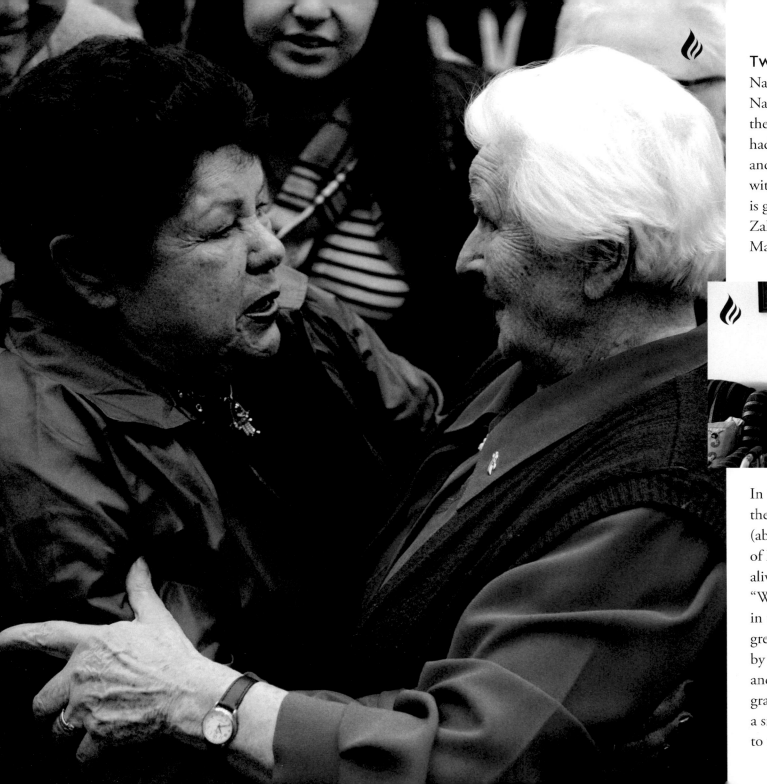

Two Dreams

Named Righteous Among the Nations for saving 14 Jews during the Shoah, Czeslawa Zak (right) had two dreams: to fly on a plane and to travel to Israel to meet with those she saved. Here she is greeted by survivor Miriam Zakrojczyka, native of Makow Mazowiecki/Krasnosielc, Poland.

In the summer of 2013, Ms. Zak – then 87 years young – met Olga Kost (above left) and the many members of her extended family who are only alive because of Czeslawa's valor. "We have managed to meet again in this world," Czeslawa said upon greeting Olga, who was surrounded by her many grandchildren and great-grandchildren. One grandchild presented Olga with a small amulet and said, "Thanks to you, we are all alive…."

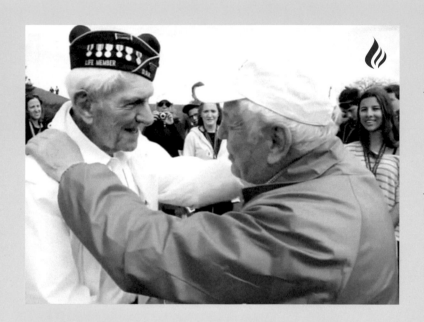

Now I Feel I Can Live Forever

Joe Mandel (right), a Holocaust survivor originally from Munkacs, Hungary, carried one regret for his entire lifetime – never thanking the American troops who liberated him. For many years, Joe never shared his Holocaust experiences with anyone, until he took part in the 2012 March of the Living. Joe's return to Eastern Europe yielded – by complete chance – a most surprising and welcome reunion with one of his liberators. Mickey Dorsey had blown open the gates to Gunnskirken 67 years earlier, and Joe was finally able to thank him. After this emotional experience, Joe said, "Now I feel I can live forever."

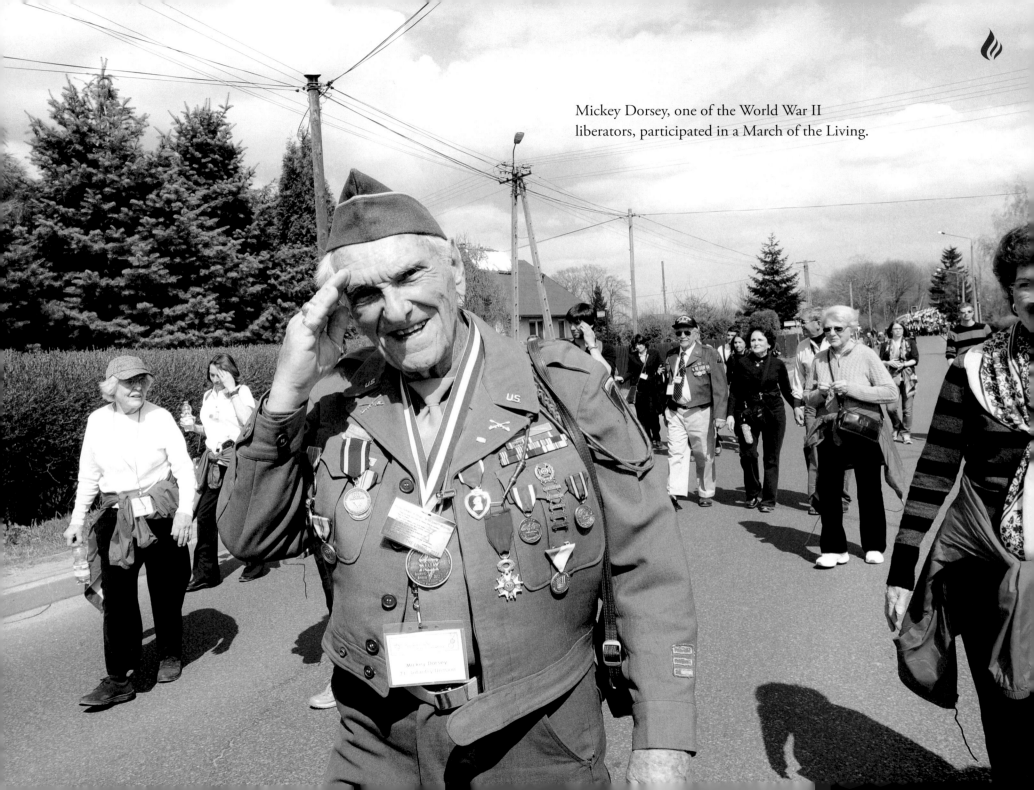

Mickey Dorsey, one of the World War II liberators, participated in a March of the Living.

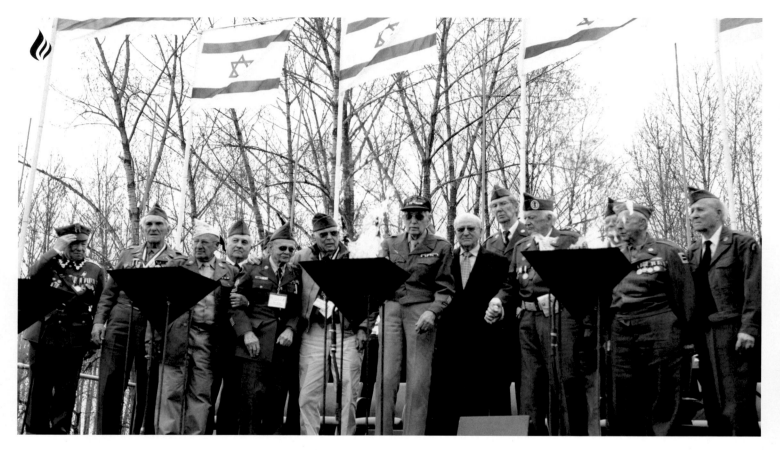

What The Messiah Looks Like

Irving Roth (in black suit and tie), is flanked by US Army WWII liberators, including Rick Carrier, the first Allied soldier to enter Buchenwald and witness the atrocities committed by the Nazis there. Irving Roth recalls that day: "By 11:00 in the morning every guard disappeared. By 3:00 in the afternoon, on April 11, 1945, Rick Carrier and his comrades came to Buchenwald. Two American soldiers walked into my building. You may not know what the Messiah looks like – but I do. There were two of them – one was black and one was white. There were 300 of us 15-year-olds weighing on average 75 pounds…skeletons! They looked at us and broke down. [But] I was free."

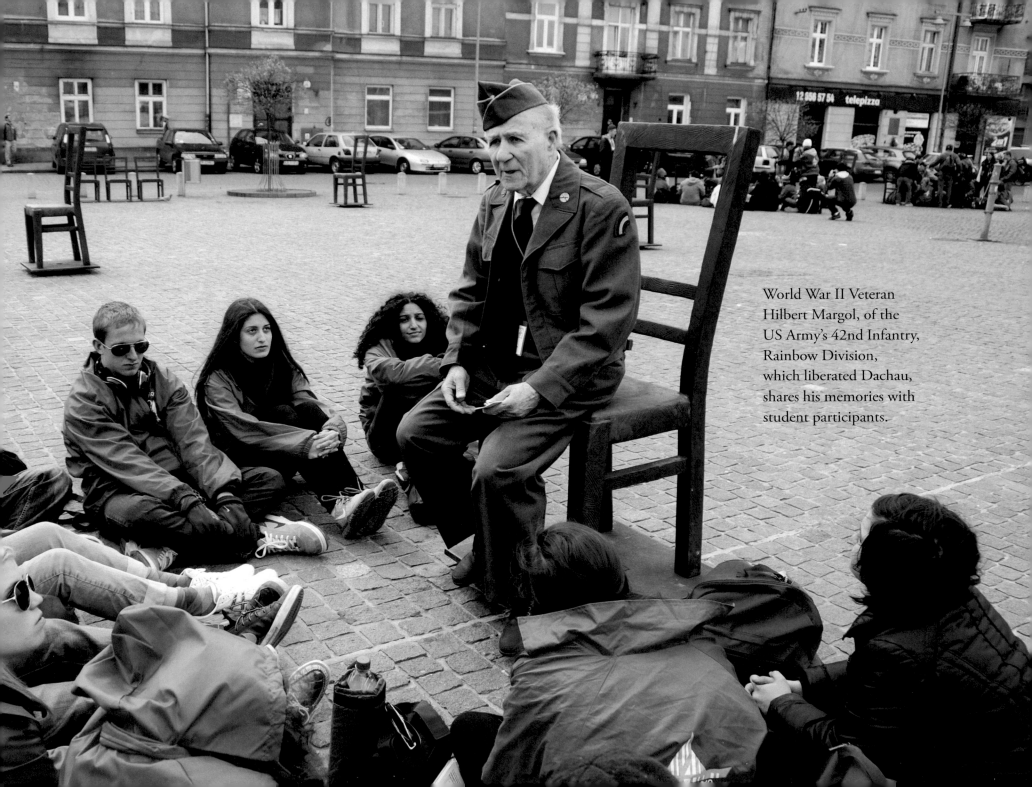

World War II Veteran
Hilbert Margol, of the
US Army's 42nd Infantry,
Rainbow Division,
which liberated Dachau,
shares his memories with
student participants.

CHAPTER FOUR

WE WHO SURVIVED

The United States Holocaust Memorial Museum defines as survivors all those "who were displaced, persecuted, or discriminated against due to the racial, religious, ethnic, and political policies of the Nazis and their allies between 1933 and 1945." Today there are approximately 350,000 Holocaust survivors still alive around the world.

Many of these survivors overcame their trauma, and began their lives again – starting new families, launching careers and founding businesses, becoming active contributors to their communities and their societies as a whole.

Yet, as any survivor will readily acknowledge, they live constantly with their tragic memories. Not a day goes by when they don't think of – and deeply miss – their lost family members and communities. In the twilight of their lives, many survivors have taken to recording their life stories, so that the memory of their family members is preserved, and so that the record of their extraordinary experiences – and the lessons to be learned from them – is not lost to future generations.

Some survivors have also been moved to record their stories because of the large number of Holocaust deniers, whose actions are a source of tremendous pain for the survivors. These deniers simultaneously refute the historical truth of one of the world's most tragic and extensively documented events, while continuing to blame the Jews for all the world's troubles, past and present. It should be remembered that in some countries – most notably Germany – Holocaust denial is treated as a crime.

In deciding to rebuild their lives, survivors demonstrate exceptional fortitude, courage, and faith. To quote Nobel Prize winner and Holocaust survivor Elie Wiesel, "To be a survivor after the Holocaust, is to have all the reason in the world to destroy and not to destroy. To have all the reasons in the world to hate and not to hate… to have all the reasons in the world to mistrust and not to mistrust. To have all the reasons in the world not to have faith in language, in singing, in prayers, not in God – but to go on telling the tale, to go on carrying on the dialogue and have our own silent prayers and quarrels with God."

Despite their disappointment in the world, most survivors did not become embittered. While many did and still do wrestle with their faith, the vast majority of survivors did not give up faith in life itself, in the capacity for

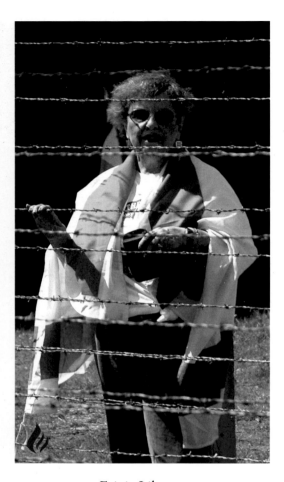

Faigie Libman at
Auschwitz-Birkenau

humanity to renew itself and to learn from past mistakes. Many of these same survivors have become eloquent spokesmen for the battle against, not just anti-Semitism, but also any kind of discrimination, racism, or intolerance.

Contemporary survivors often echo the same sentiment. When society pushes people to its fringes, when it mistreats the marginalized and the disenfranchised – be they immigrants or people with disabilities or a different skin color – they are among the first to raise their voices, saying, "We the survivors have been there, we above all people know what that feels like, and we know the terrible path down which these behaviors can lead us. Let us not repeat the same moral tragedy."

The survivors who are with us today serve three significant roles, among others:

Storytellers: Survivors are repositories of the stories that reflect one of the most cataclysmic moral failures in the history of humanity.

Teachers: Survivors are often the voices of moral clarity, modern-day and eloquent prophets who teach us of our civic duties and our responsibilities toward our fellow human beings – and how we so often have failed them.

Models of Resilience: Survivors remind us that human beings have the capacity to rebuild their lives after having experienced the most devastating of losses imaginable.

In every country where they found themselves after the war, survivors made their mark. They are the ultimate example of the ability of love to overcome darkness, of faith to overcome adversity, of hope to overcome despair. Perhaps Holocaust survivor Faigie Libman, standing in Poland with a group of young people from Canada, the US, and Australia, summed up best what many survivors feel when she said: "When you have hatred in your heart, there is no room for love."

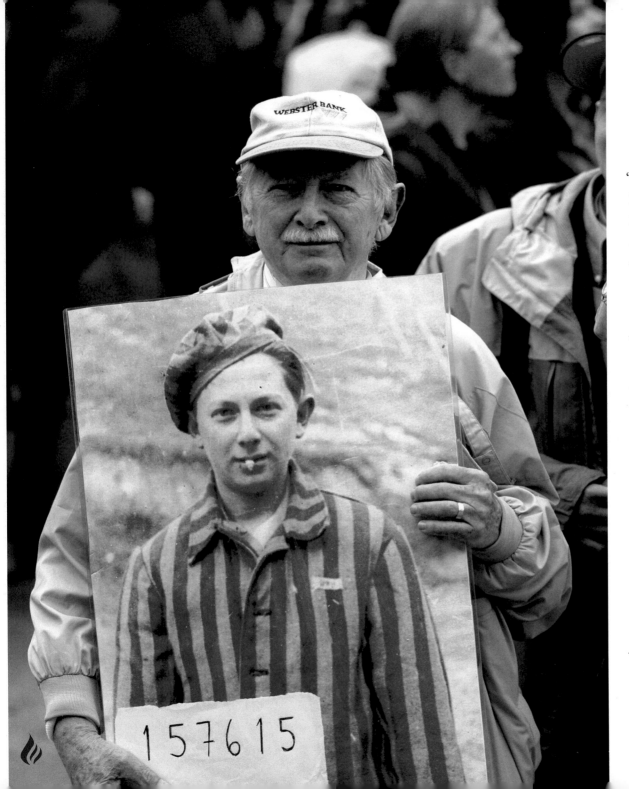

Prisoner 157615

"My father, Icek (Irving) Cymbler from Zawiercie, Poland, was prisoner number 157615. That number was tattooed on his arm. He was 15 when he arrived in Auschwitz, but he lied about his age. As a result, he was not gassed, as his parents and three sisters eventually were. Instead, he was sent to a slave labor camp in Warsaw. In August 1944, he was sent on a Death March to Dachau. On April 30, 1945, the US Army liberated him as he rode a train headed to the Tyrolean Mountains. The Nazis were waiting there to execute him and his fellow prisoners.

"In 2008, my father returned with me to Auschwitz-Birkenau on the March of the Living. He had a photo of himself in his Dachau prisoner uniform taken a year after the liberation. I had an enlargement made and he held it proudly as we marched in Auschwitz. He had survived.

"My father passed away in 2011, two days shy of his 84th birthday. I miss him."
—Jeffrey Cymbler

Do Not Create the Same Hatred That Was Done to Us

Max Glauben was born in Warsaw, Poland, in 1928. During the war, he survived the Warsaw Ghetto and several camps including Majdanek (where much of his family perished), Budzyn, and Flossenburg, before he was liberated on April 23, 1945. He has returned to Poland on the March of the Living eight times, sharing his difficult story with young students in a way that he hopes will encourage them to build a better world for all humanity. As he says, "I am a strong believer that we must tell the stories to the youngsters – they are going to be our witnesses. But please present them in a way, with the kind of emotions, that will not create the same hatred that was done to us."

The 2012 March of the Living was especially significant to Max, when he saw the group of blind participants with their guide dogs. "When I saw the dogs, I wanted to honor the courage these blind people had to come on a trip like this. It so touched my heart to see that the same animals used by the Nazis to maim us are now helping us, here in this very spot."

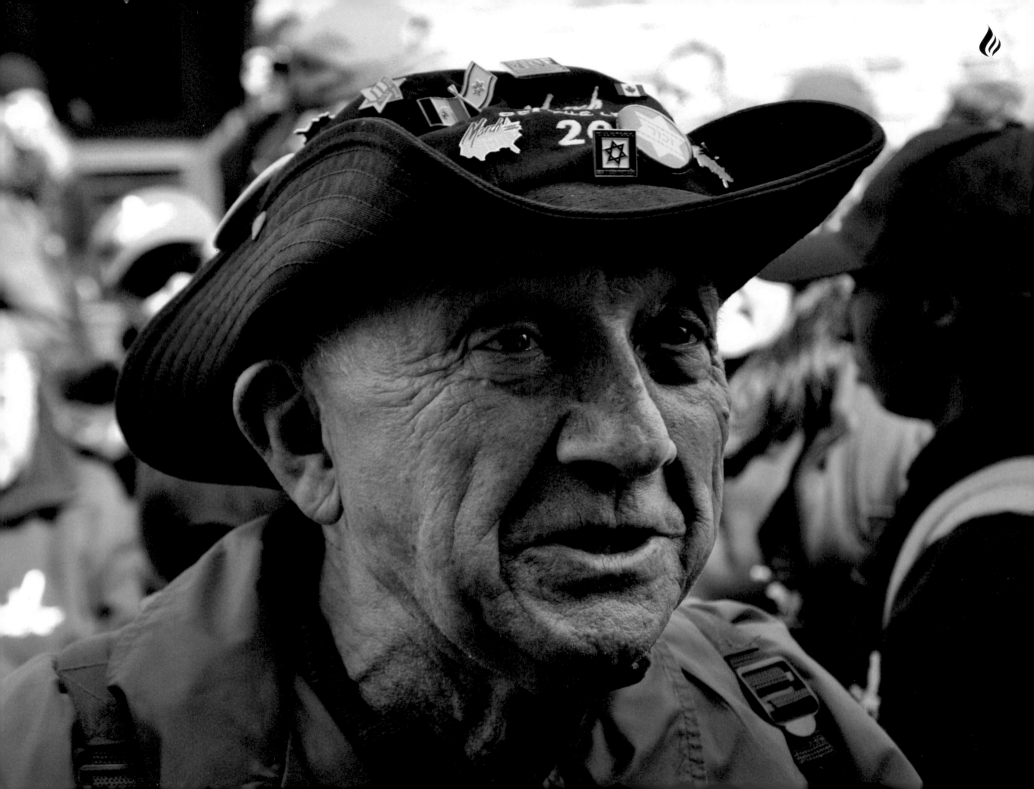

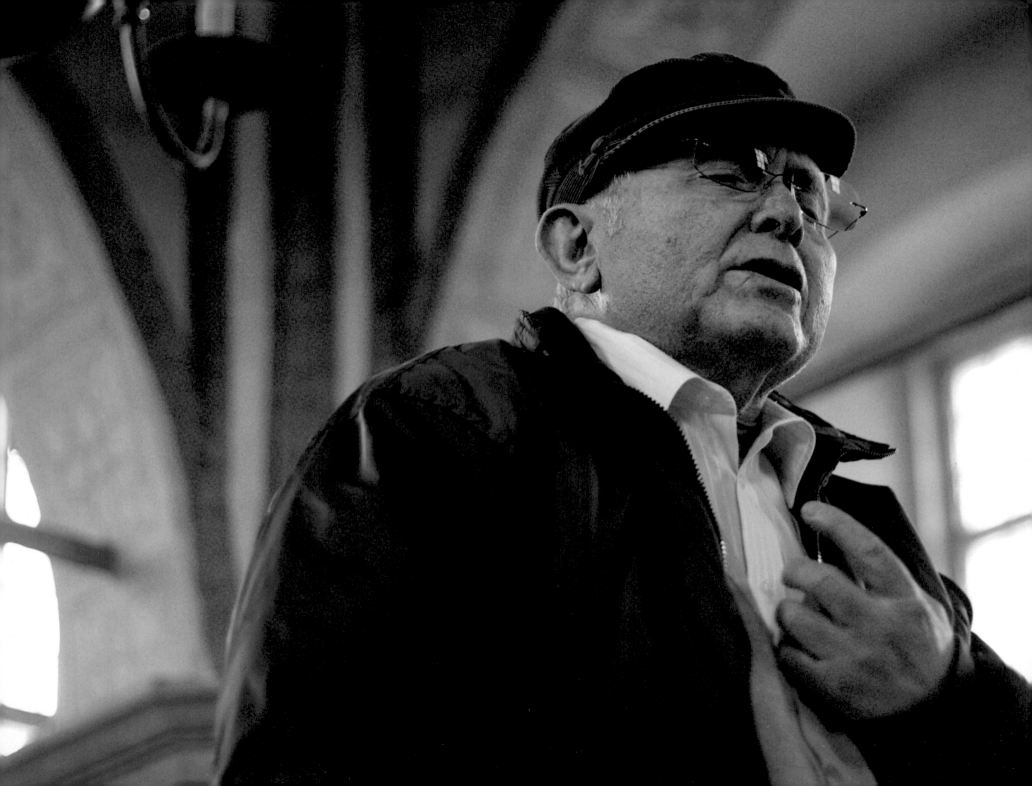

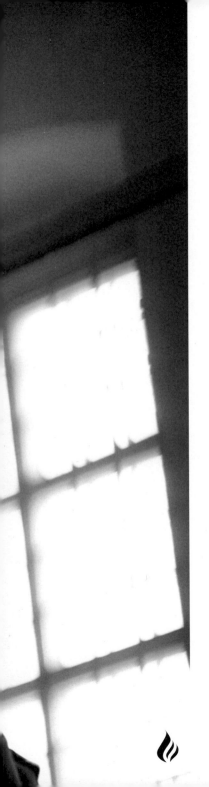

Drop By Drop By Drop

Holocaust survivor Pinchas Gutter chanted a traditional prayer in a restored synagogue in the village of Tykocin in northeastern Poland. "I always tell the young that I am carrying a torch of well-being and goodness. Despite the fact that it could have been a bitter one, I believe that my torch should be like the Olympic torch, a torch that brings goodwill on Earth.

"We had a person named Moses on our trip, a survivor of the genocide in Rwanda. It was incredible how he bonded with me, by my being able to tell my stories. He wrote a letter about how it's much easier for him to accept, to live in the future because I have given him another *Weltanschauung*, another worldview. It's very important for Holocaust survivors – or anybody else – to spread togetherness and goodwill and I think it's the young people specifically who can create this. Because drop, by drop, by drop, like water on a stone, the world can become a better place."

At the 20th anniversary dinner of the USC Shoah Foundation in Los Angeles on May 7, 2014, President Barack Obama had this to say:

"I think of Pinchas Gutter, a man who lived through the Warsaw Ghetto Uprising, and survived the Majdanek death camp… 'I tell my story,' he says, 'for the purpose of improving humanity, drop by drop by drop. Like a drop of water falls on a stone and erodes it, so, hopefully, by telling my story over and over again, I will achieve the purpose of making the world a better place to live in.' Those are the words of one survivor – performing that sacred duty of memory – that will echo throughout eternity. Those are good words for all of us to live by."

"Triumph does not erase the memories of a tragedy. It does not mend the scars that were left behind nor does it bring back what was forever lost."
—Quoted by Hannah Berdowski, 16, March of the Living, 2012

SURVIVORS

"Survivors", they say, I say "ha."

"Survivors" of the Holocaust?

Survivors of Death, maybe

but the Holocaust? No,

No one *survived* the Holocaust.

We see reminders – train tracks, sheds,

old bowls, clothes, pictures, books, eyes.

We see the eyes of survivors.

—Miriam Naylor, 20, March of the Living, 1990

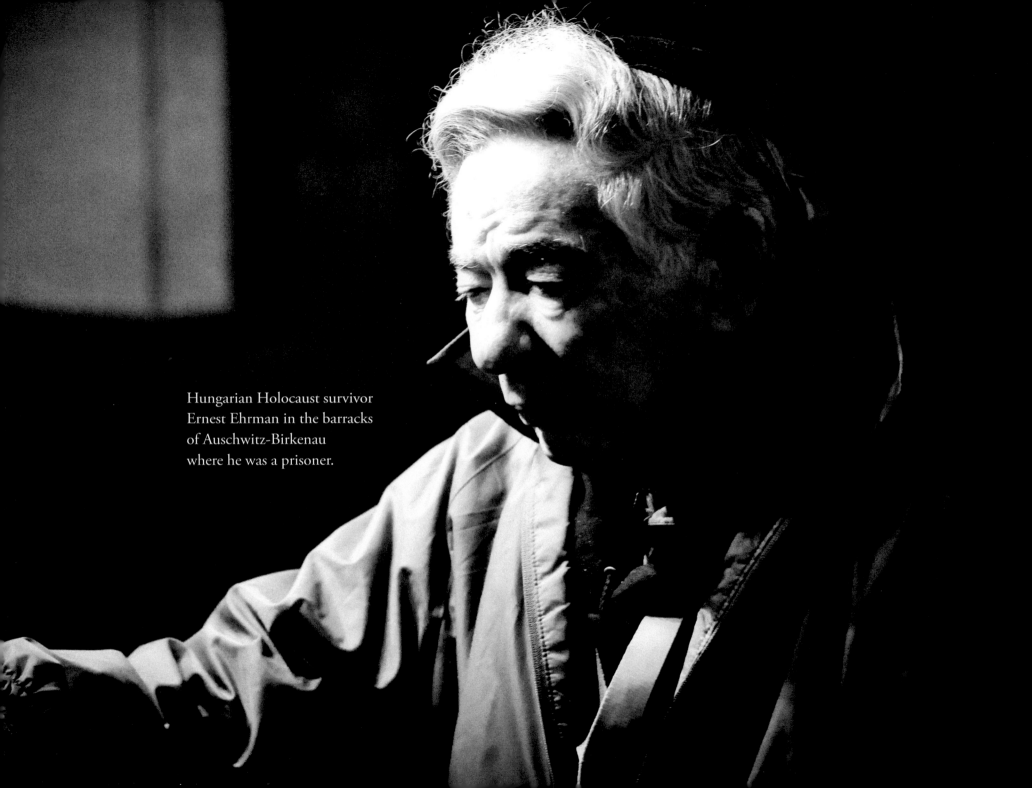

Hungarian Holocaust survivor
Ernest Ehrman in the barracks
of Auschwitz-Birkenau
where he was a prisoner.

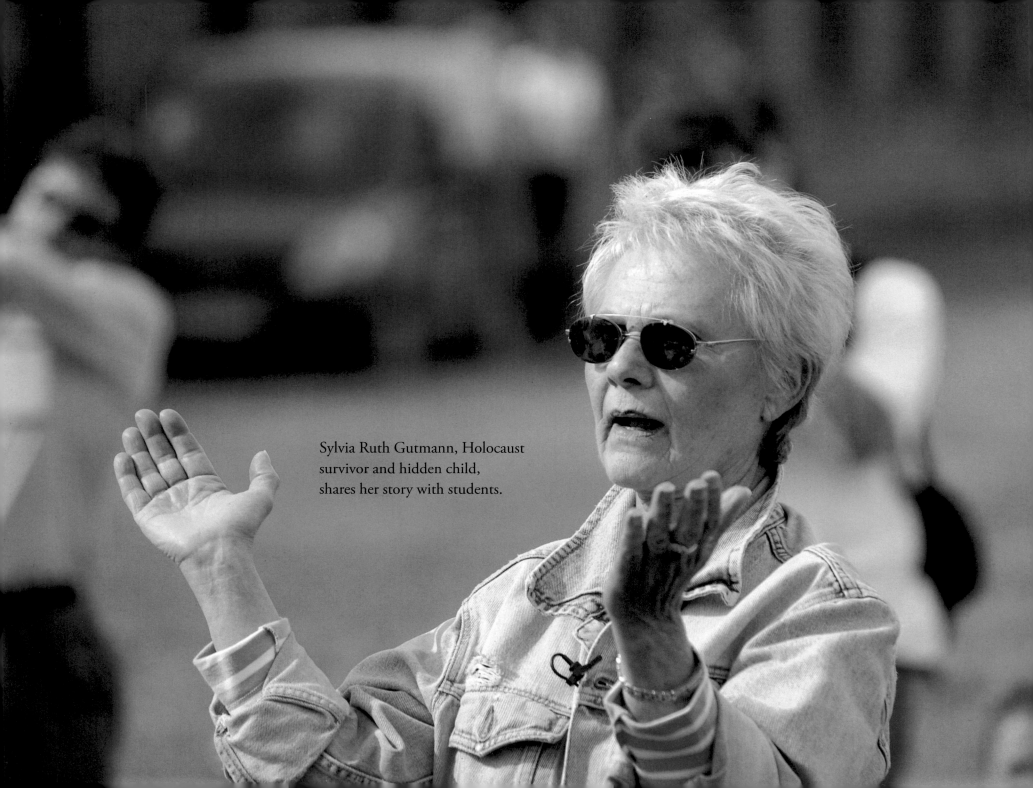

Sylvia Ruth Gutmann, Holocaust survivor and hidden child, shares her story with students.

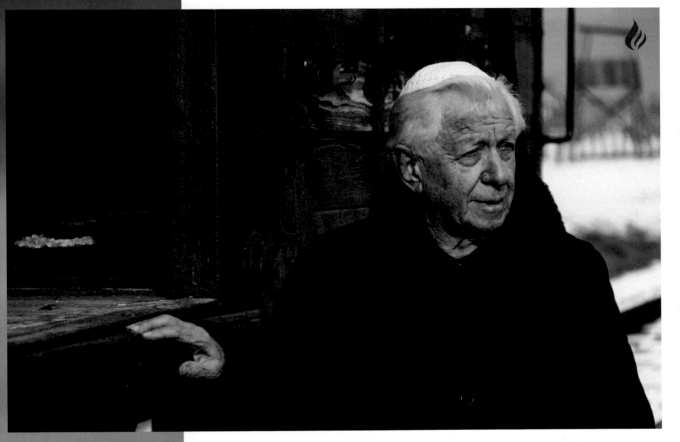

For more than half a century what happened to Frank Lowy's beloved father was a mystery. A chance meeting with another Holocaust survivor – the last person to see Frank's father alive – revealed his tragic, yet heroic fate. He was beaten to death by the guards for standing up for his religion and for refusing to relinquish his articles of faith.

Under This Same Sky

Frank Lowy related his story to participants on a March of the Living standing in front of a cattle car used to transport Jews to Auschwitz-Birkenau.

"A few months after my Bar Mitzvah, my father disappeared. I waited for almost fifty years [to find out what happened to him]. In all that time, I never forgot him. Even in my dreams. So here I am, with you all in Birkenau. I know he was also here, under this same sky. Just like almost half a million Hungarian Jews, he came to this place in a wagon, and almost immediately after arriving, disappeared as smoke into this sky. I was 13 when I lost my father and now I am 82 – and you know, I still miss him.... I still feel the loss of my father. But there is something I have gained. I never realized that he had strength – the spiritual strength – to take on the brutal guards here. No matter how hard they hit him, he protected the sanctity of his tallit and tefillin [religious objects]. They could break his body but they could not break his spirit. The tallit and tefillin were part of him, part of his personal relationship with God. He was ready to die for them. *And he did.*"

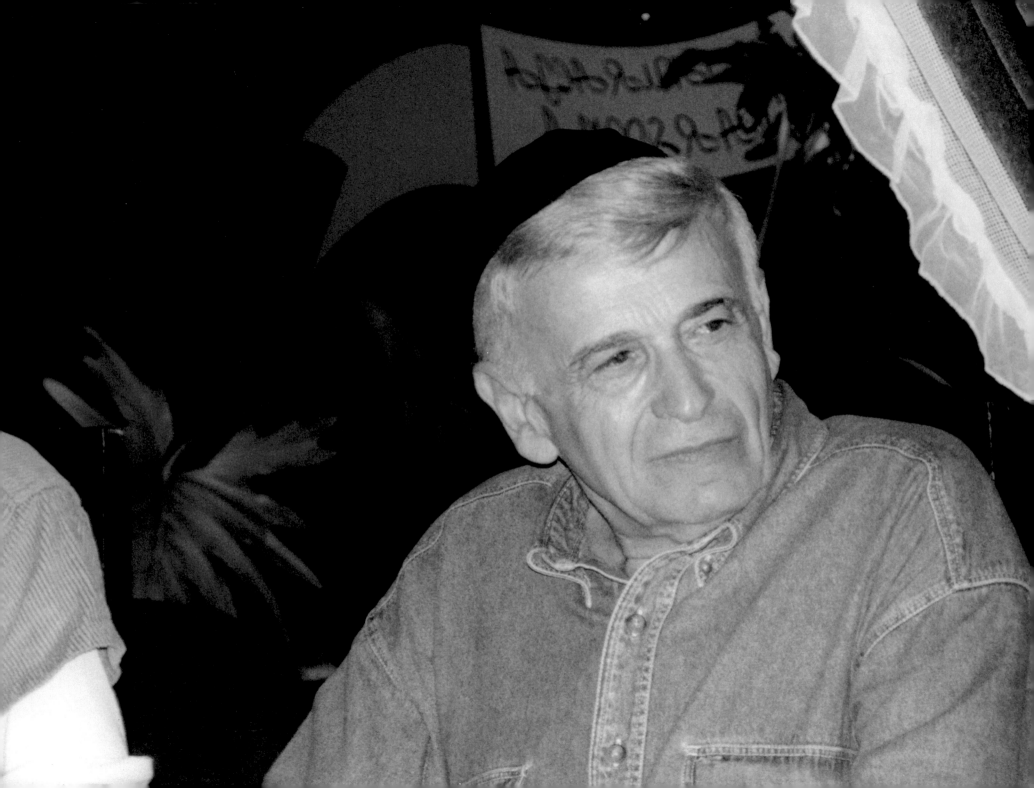

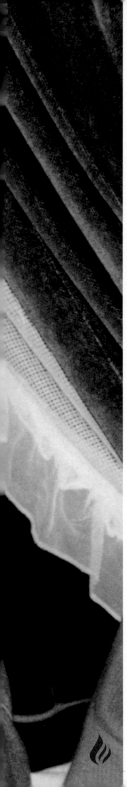

Like a Hand Reaching Out

One freezing night – on January 18, 1945 – 15-year-old Jewish prisoner Max Eisen was forced to march out of Auschwitz, herded at gunpoint by SS guards with dogs. The prisoners were wearing wooden clogs and were slipping in the snow. Many prisoners were shot when they could not keep up the pace or had dropped out from exhaustion. Max walked for four or five days without food or water, only managing to pick up a few handfuls of snow for moisture on the way.

Eventually, they were loaded onto open metal boxcars, whose sides were so cold they almost froze to the metal. When the boxcar arrived in Pilsen, some kindly Czech people appeared on the overhead bridge and began to throw pieces of bread into the open boxcars. The guards shouted: "Don't throw any bread. These are Jews." But the people just kept on throwing bread into the boxcars below until the guards started to shoot at them. For Max, even though he was too far away to snatch any of the bread, this was one of the most important moments of his life. After all he had been through, to learn there were still decent people left in the world – this began to restore the boy's faith in the world. "It was like a hand reaching out to me," Max tells the students. He never forgot the goodness of the people of Pilsen, for whom he felt a debt of gratitude every day of his life.

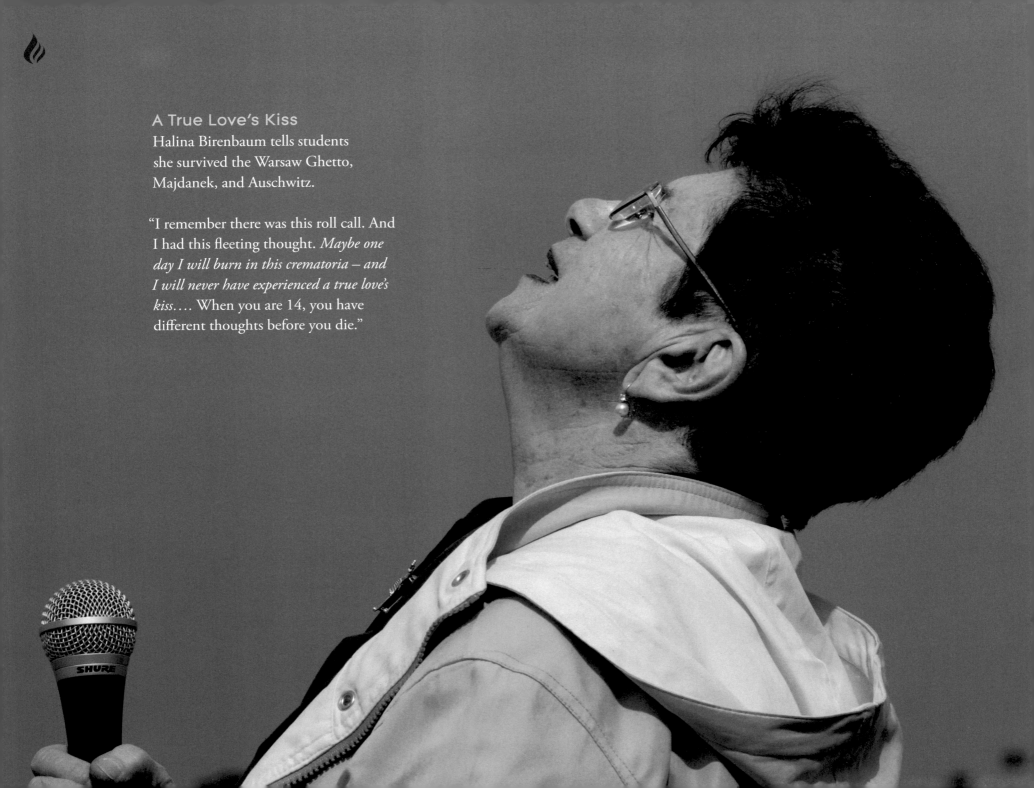

A True Love's Kiss

Halina Birenbaum tells students she survived the Warsaw Ghetto, Majdanek, and Auschwitz.

"I remember there was this roll call. And I had this fleeting thought. *Maybe one day I will burn in this crematoria – and I will never have experienced a true love's kiss.…* When you are 14, you have different thoughts before you die."

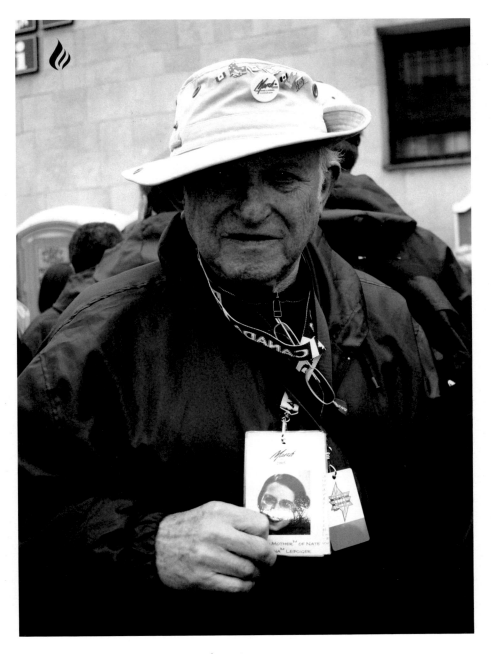

Nate Leipciger, Holocaust survivor, marched in memory of his mother.

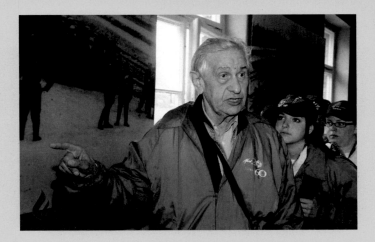

Why I March, Why I Speak

Holocaust survivor David Shentow explains to students that when he first learned there were people today denying the Holocaust – denying all the suffering he went through – "I said there and then, I would crawl on my hands and knees all the way to Auschwitz-Birkenau, or anywhere else, to tell my story to anyone who was willing to listen. This is why I march and why I still speak."

We Will Walk In Together
We Will Walk Out Together

"Well, when we went to Auschwitz…it shook me up. Especially when I saw the big sign [*Arbeit Mach Frei*]. It brought back such painful memories. I just stood at the gate. I was mesmerized. [Then] one student came up to me, 'David, David…we will walk in together, and we will walk out together.'

"They were holding on to me or I was holding on to them. I don't remember anymore – the sympathy, the hugging…there are no words to describe it. It will be with me forever."

CHAPTER FIVE

SURVIVORS AND STUDENTS:
PASSING THE TORCH OF MEMORY

Since the fall of the Iron Curtain, large numbers of students and Holocaust survivors have returned to the killing fields of Eastern Europe to encounter the Holocaust and other WWII genocides in the very places these tragic events transpired.

These young people and their aging mentors come thousands of miles from their homes and, with their own two feet, tread upon the very earth where so many of their ancestors prayed, loved – and perished. This act of travelling to these former places of life and learning, destruction and martyrdom, is in itself a cry of protest over the injustices of the past. It is an act of sacred memorialization, a statement to the entire world – and perhaps even to those who have perished – that the martyrdom of so many millions will never be forgotten.

The students who participate are not just learning about history, but, with their physical presence, they also are touching and indeed entering history. They make a statement with their entire being, in the present, about the past.

Sally Wasserman, a Holocaust survivor and hidden child, from Poland, recalled one moment from all her March of the Living trips that still stands out for her. She and her students had visited a lovely town called Tykocin, a *shtetl* right out of *Fiddler on the Roof*. The synagogue in the village square, dating back to 1642, had been lovingly restored and was a reminder of the traditional way of life that once thrived there. The group then left the idyllic town and traveled to the nearby Lupochowa forest, where the Jews of the town were marched into the forest in August 1941, ordered to dig pits, then shot en masse into the graves they had been forced to prepare for themselves. Silence engulfed the students standing at this somber site of grievous carnage. "I'm not a religious person," Sally recalled, "but I couldn't help myself. I shouted, 'Please, please, someone say a *Kaddish*.'" (Jewish memorial prayer for the dead.) The prayer was recited in the middle of the lush green forest that hid this terrible crime. And everyone answered "Amen."

Why do we return? We come to say, "We are here, and with all our might and all our strength, we proclaim on this very ground, with our bodies and our souls: We remember, we shall always remember." And to answer Amen when a prayer is recited in the memory of so many martyrs.

The single most significant aspect of these pilgrimages is the role of the survivors, who share their painful Holocaust experiences with the students in the very places their stories unfolded. Over the years, thousands of stories have been transmitted by survivors to students in Europe – standing near the dome of ashes in Majdanek, or in a barracks, or the ramp in Auschwitz, or in a synagogue in Kraków, or near the wall of names in Belzec, or the silent stone markers in Treblinka. Each story is more heartbreaking than the last, each a story of life and love interrupted, of irreparable loss.

Who can forget Pinchas Gutter telling of the last time he saw his twin sister in Majdanek? All he can remember is the long, golden-blonde braid swinging behind her back as she was herded with their mother to her end. He cannot, try as he might, recall her face.

And how could anyone forget Judy Weissenberg Cohen telling of the last time she saw her mother, during the selection on the train tracks in Birkenau, and how, to this day, she still wishes she had given her mother one last hug and kiss good-bye.

Which student could ever forget Anita Ekstein, whose life was saved by righteous Poles, visiting Belzec on, of all days, Mother's Day and finding her mother's name on the memorial wall in the Belzec death camp. Or the recounting of her father's last words to her, his 8-year-old daughter: "Always remember who you are."

And yet, in the survivors' act of telling, of transmitting their memories to a new generation, a new seed of hope is planted. In the act of embarking on these trips, the young people are, in effect, pledging this: "Your struggles will be remembered and your loved ones will not be forgotten. We, a new generation of young people, commit to creating a better world for all humanity, a world far different than the one that sought to destroy your generation."

The Holocaust literally shattered our world. We who were born in the post-Holocaust era have inherited a broken world. For many, the Holocaust still challenges their faith in God, their faith in humanity, or in both.

But as we study this broken world of ours, and then look at the earnest faces of our young people, who so much want to understand, to make a difference, to not repeat the mistakes of the past, we are reminded of what a Jewish mystic taught us some two centuries ago: If you believe it can be broken, then know it can also be fixed.

Each time we return to Poland, each time a Holocaust survivor shares his or her story of survival, we are denying Hitler's aims; each time survivors share the stories of their martyred relatives, we are lifting them from their anonymous deaths, and denying Hitler a posthumous victory. Each time a group of young people arrives in Auschwitz and proclaims the values of human dignity and equality, we know our broken world can yet again be made whole.

Looking out on the sea of humanity, upon thousands of young people from around the world, marching from Auschwitz to Birkenau on Holocaust Remembrance Day, Anita Ekstein told her daughter Ruth, "You see? Hitler did not win."

Our Holocaust survivors and our young people have banded together to remind the world of the terrible wave of hatred that once engulfed it, and how we must strive to set a new course for humanity, one that embraces love, dignity, and empathy for each and every member of the human family.

Their legacy is our hope.

MARCH ON
It's hard to walk on in their shoes, the shoes
we saw at Majdanek.
Me, without scars – in the scraped up shoes,
dirty, soft, and old.
But new for me. It's hard to decide when to
put them on –
And when to take them off.
—Marni Levitt, 15, March of the Living, 1990

The Last Time I Saw my Mother

"I never had a chance to say good-bye to my mother. We didn't know we had to say good-bye.
…I am an old woman today and I never made peace with the fact that I never had that last hug and kiss. They say, 'When you listen to a witness, you become a witness.' I am only asking you to work for a world where nobody will have to live with memories like mine ever again. Please heal the world."

Judy Weissenberg Cohen, a Hungarian Holocaust survivor, shares her story with her young students in Auschwitz-Birkenau on a March of the Living.

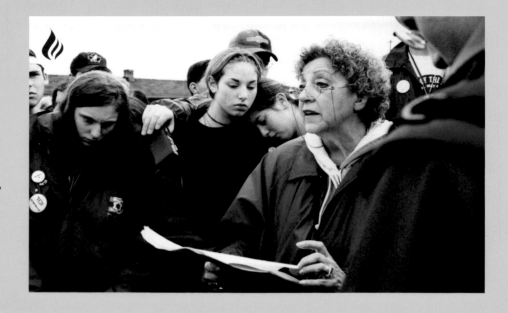

March of the Living students accompanied Holocaust survivor Lillian Boraks-Nemetz on a visit to the small Polish village of Zalesie, where she was hidden during the war.

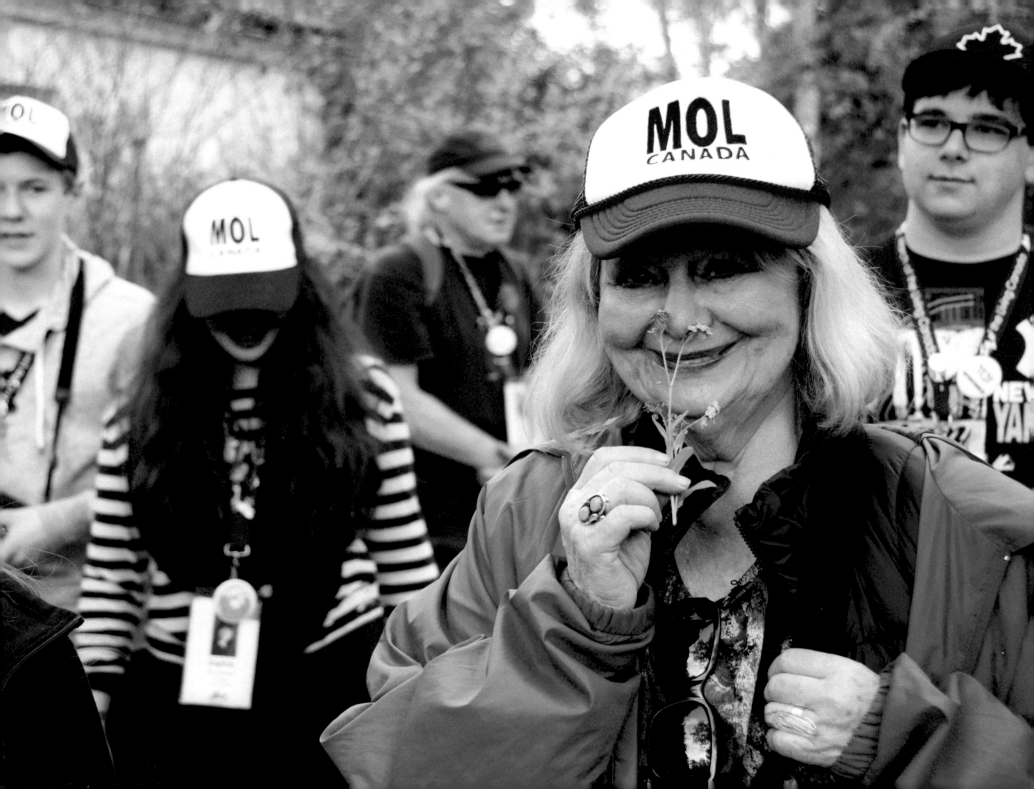

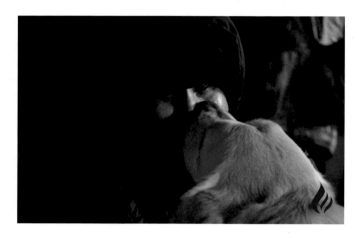

Guide dog Petel licks tears from Liron Artzi's face after an emotional moment in the former Majdanek Gas Chamber.

Blind Love and Blind Hate

Liron Artzi, a blind participant on the 2012 March of the Living, wrote to her guide dog, Petel (Raspberry), after their experience on the trip.

Dear Petel,

You were with me in the Jewish cemetery, at the walls of the Warsaw Ghetto and in the frozen forest where the shooting pits were found, at the synagogues, and in Treblinka-Majdanek-Auschwitz.

You were there during all of this and couldn't speak. But your love for me I felt in every lick, every time I stroked you, every time you came and placed your head on my knees.

Petel, I always say that you are in my heart. This time you entered straight into my soul, you are part of my blood, part of me, forever.

These words were written directly from the heart to a (guide) dog that is one big heart.

Liron

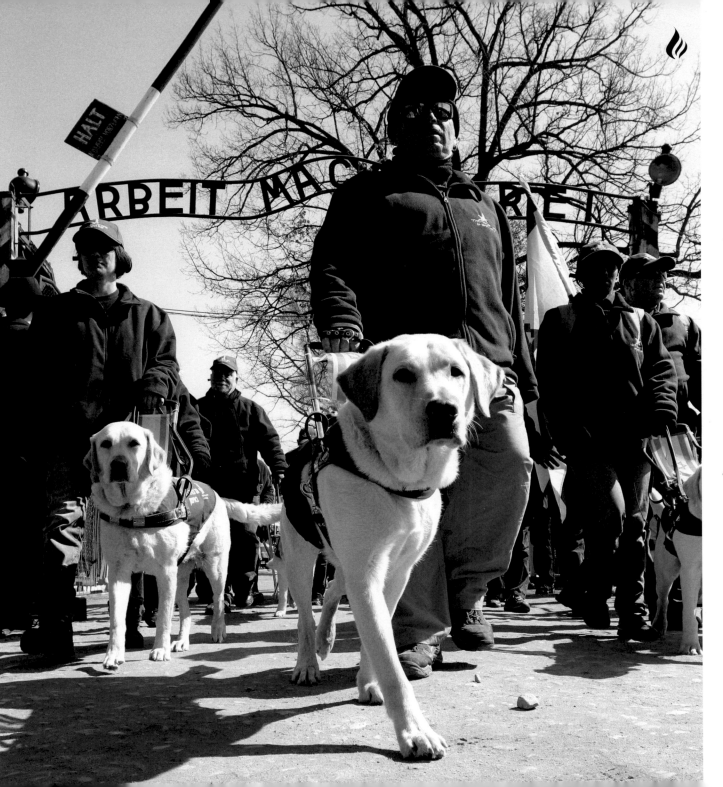

Leaving the Gates of Auschwitz

Blind delegates from Israel leave the gates of Auschwitz with their guide dogs. The Nazis murdered not only Jews, but also people with disabilities, often using viciously trained dogs to terrorize prisoners. The sign on the entrance gate above them reads: *Arbeit Macht Frei* (Work makes you free), the cynical Nazi slogan used to deceive arriving prisoners about the ultimate purpose of the camp.

"It's love, not work, that sets us free," stated David Matlow, a 2015 March of the Living participant. He was referencing the last line of "Lay Down Your Arms," a peace song sung by the March of the Living students in Auschwitz, which concludes with the words, "And love will someday set us free."

Sylvia Ruth
Gutmann clasps
the hand of
an American
Muslim student at
Auschwitz-Birkenau
on the March of
Remembrance
and Hope.

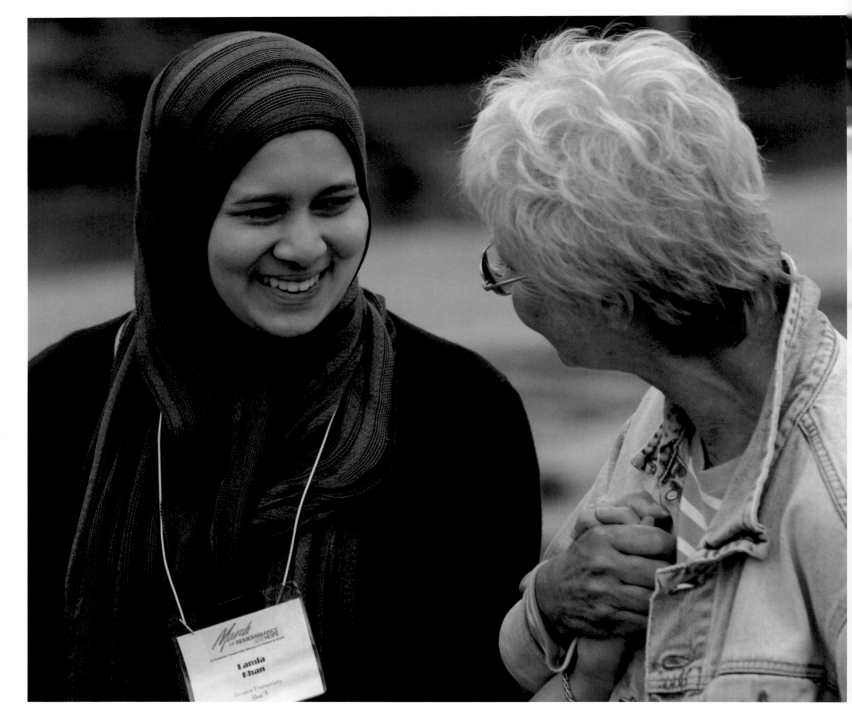

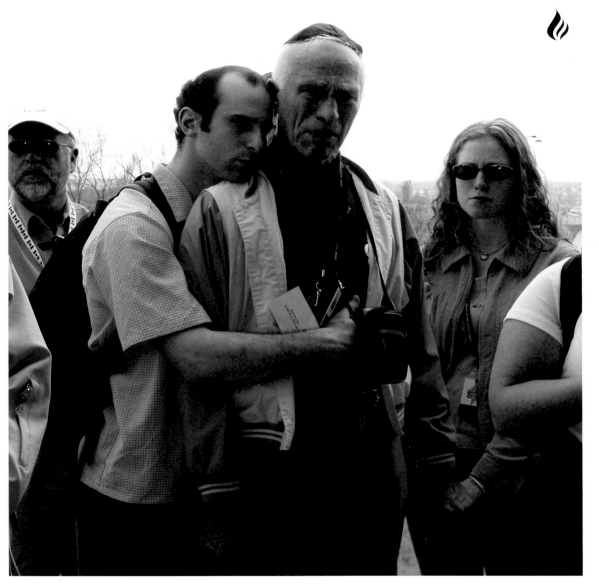

Here

"We were marching in Auschwitz-Birkenau, and we saw Max was alone. So we decided to go over to comfort him. We each took one of his strong arms – and marched with him. As we approached the gates, I asked him: 'What happened to your family?'

"He stopped, his eyes filled with tears, and he just pointed down. He said one word: 'Here.' That's all he had to say – we knew. 'Here' was where his family was murdered."
—Aria Smorden, 15,
March of the Living, 2013

Max Iland, a teacher from Sault Ste. Marie, Ontario, is surrounded and comforted by his children, Yaacov and Hannah, in Auschwitz-Birkenau where Max's mother and his 3-year-old brother, Kopel, were murdered.

A Dialogue

Nate Leipciger: "You cannot have hate in your heart without being hateful against yourself. And that's the big problem – when you are hateful, you become bitter, you resent everything and that becomes part of your nature."

Student: "You don't hate the soldiers, who took those kids out [and murdered them]?"

Nate Leipciger: "There is a difference between hating and holding them responsible. They are two different feelings. I don't have to like them, but I don't hate them. Because hate will destroy the person doing the hating."

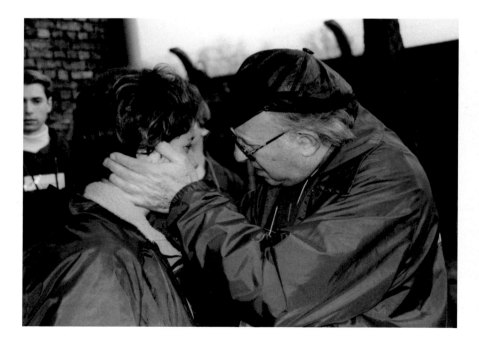

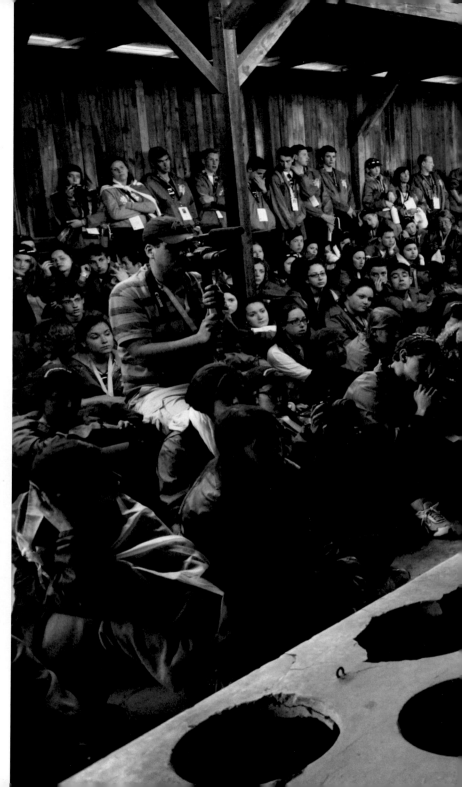

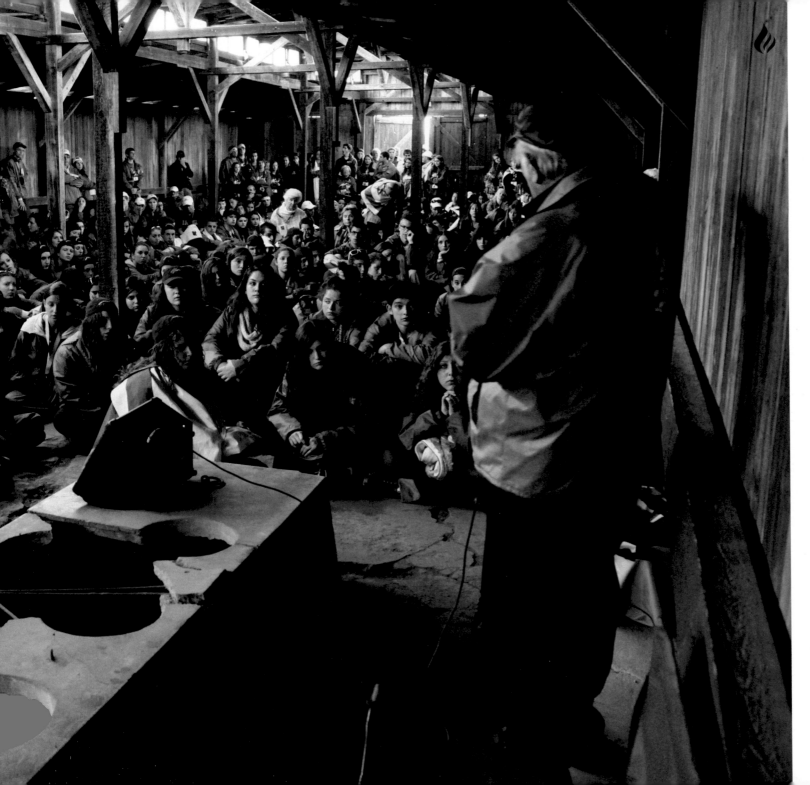

Nate Liepciger holds the attention of rapt students in one of the barracks in Auschwitz-Birkenau. Born in Poland in 1928, he survived the Sosnowiec Ghetto and the camps of Auschwitz-Birkenau, where he was a former inmate. He told students that each day was a struggle for survival. Prisoners were housed in barracks that were not insulated from the heat or cold. Prisoners were allowed to use the primitive latrine only once daily. A barrack held as many as 500 inmates who were squeezed five or six across into wooden bunks.

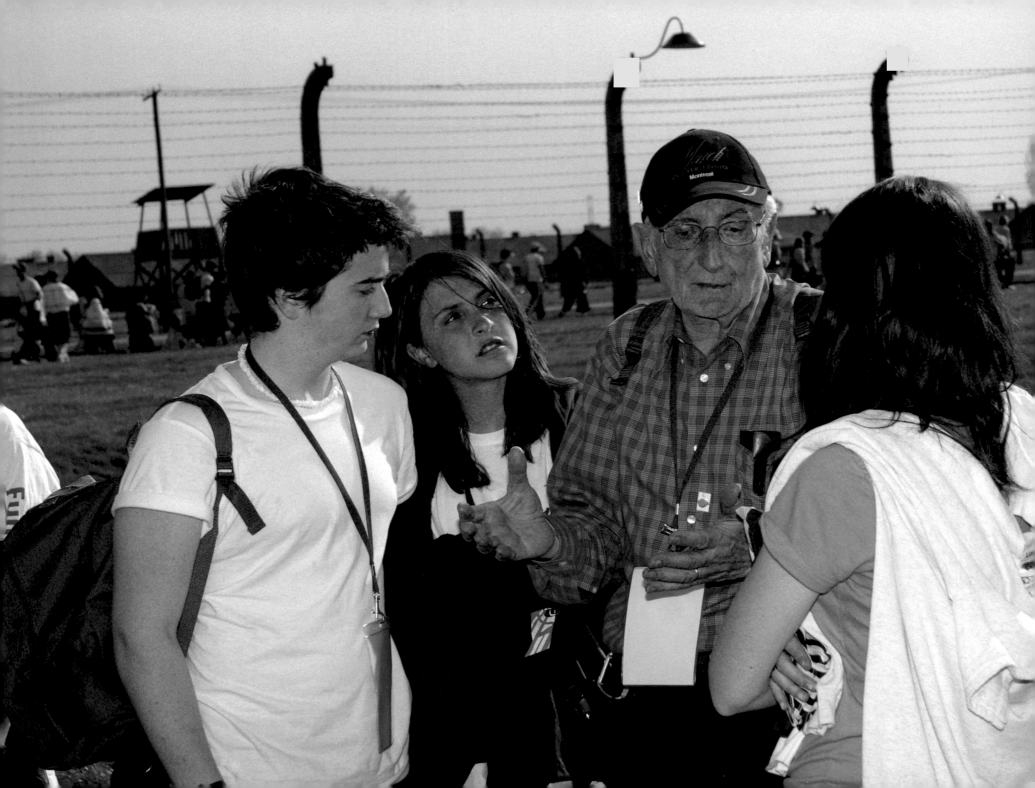

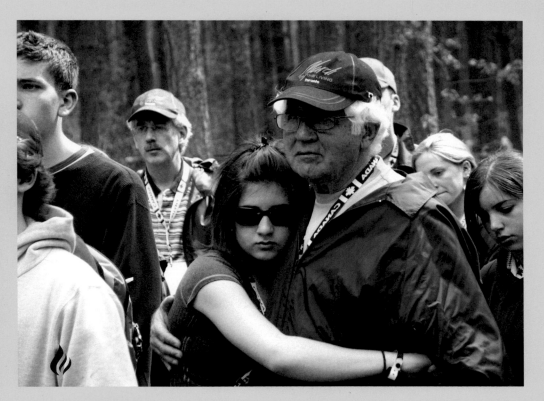

Bill Glied (pictured with his granddaughter on the March of the Living) was born in Subotica, Serbia, and deported to Auschwitz-Birkenau in April 1944 with his entire family. He never saw his mother or sister again. "They just disappeared from my life – I didn't get to say good-bye."

Stones of Memory

"There is a unique and noble custom in the Jewish religion. We go to the cemetery and find the graves of our loved ones. Then we take a small stone and place it on the tombstone to say, 'We are here. We haven't forgotten you. We love you. We remember you.'

"In Auschwitz there are no tombstones. All those who perished here – my mother, my sister, my whole family – they have no monuments. But all of you who are standing here today, you are the little stones, and you are saying, 'We are here. We haven't forgotten you. We love you.'"
—Bill Glied,
March of the Living, 2009

Mayer Schondorf shared his story with teen students on the March of the Living in Auschwitz-Birkenau. Mayer died in 2009.

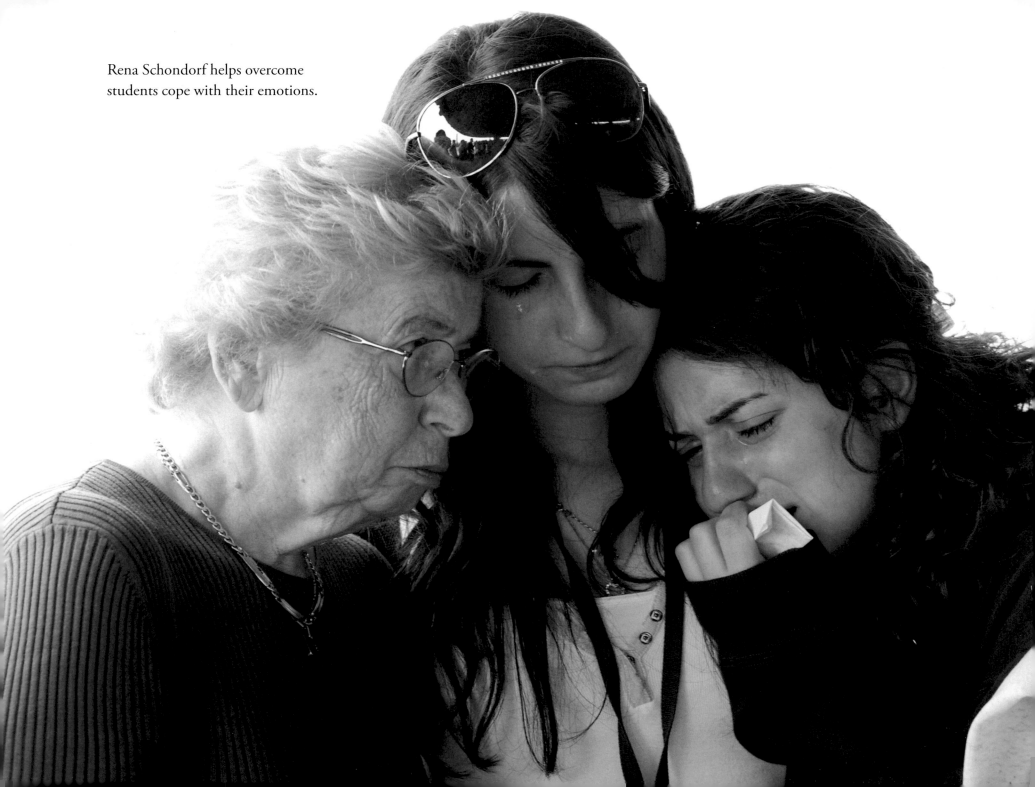

Rena Schondorf helps overcome
students cope with their emotions.

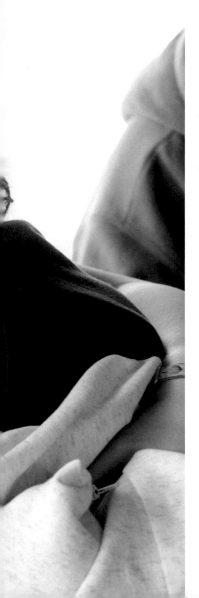

NOT EVER AGAIN
The hands that clasped mine,
the arms that embraced me,
the tears that mingled with mine
strengthened me and gave me hope
in those very places where for many
hope had once failed.
Not this time. Not ever again.
That was what I learned.
And that was what the marchers learned.
We did not return unchanged.
—Harold Lass, March of the Living, 1990

I Was a Lonely Rock

Asher Aud was 12 years old when his father and older brother were deported from the ghetto of their Polish town, Zdunska Wola, near Lodz. Two years later, his mother and younger brother were murdered in Chelmno. Now on his own, the 14-year-old was sent to Lodz Ghetto.

"From the moment I was separated from my mother, I was a lonely rock. I didn't have friends, I didn't have anyone…. There were no days of the week, no Monday or Tuesday, all the days were the same." In August 1944, Aud was deported to Camp E, Block 4 at Auschwitz. There he found his older brother, Berl, who helped him survive the brutal camp. In January 1945, 17-year-old Asher Aud was sent on a Death March, finding himself in Mauthausen and Gunskirchen before being liberated and immigrating to Israel. Almost 40 years later he was reunited with his brother.

"How did a young boy survive this? I went through it," Aud says, "but can't explain it. I wanted only one thing: I wanted to live. There was nothing else, just the desire to live.

"I didn't talk about the Holocaust for more than 50 years. It wasn't that I wanted to forget, but there were no social workers, no psychologists to tell us how to act after this. If we wanted to live, we couldn't talk about it. To talk is to live it…. Then, following a visit to Poland, I told my story for the first time. In light of all the Holocaust denial, I came to the conclusion that anyone who could talk must! The impact is very different; I see and hear its effect in the responses from the students."

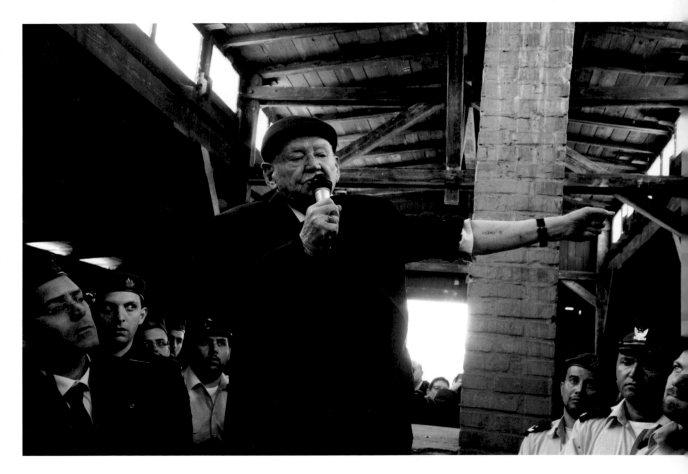

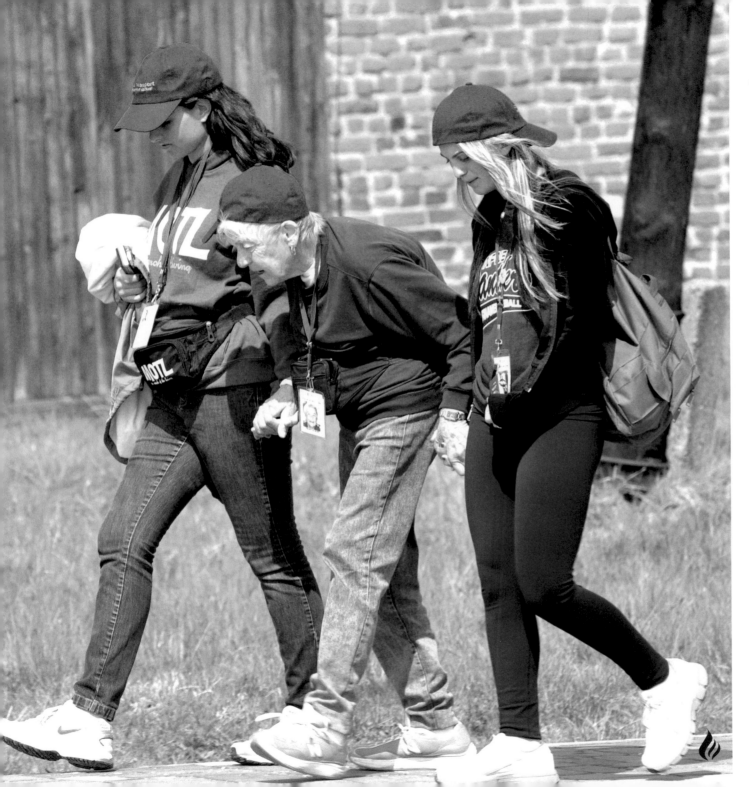

You Become our Survivors

"Hearing my story, you young people become, in a way, our survivors. You must never, ever let this memory die – you must keep the torch burning. Because one day my generation will pass. Then, in your lifetime, when you hear someone say that the Holocaust did not happen, you can say: 'I met a woman who was in Auschwitz and survived Auschwitz. The Holocaust did happen because this person lost her entire family in it – her two sisters, her mother and father. And so did six million other Jews, along with gypsies, the disabled, Christians who tried to save Jews, gays, and many others.' As a survivor of 70 years, when I see what the world is like today [I fear] we have not learned much from the past. People are suppressing other people. The best way to honor those who perished is to *educate* the future generations. We must ensure that these atrocities never happen to any other human being."

Trudy Album, Holocaust survivor from Hungary/Czechoslovakia, accompanied by two students on the March of the Living, where she shared her experiences.

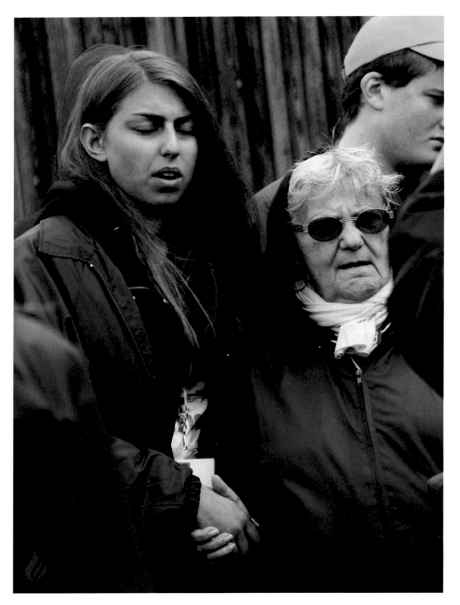
Sally Wasserman with students at Auschwitz-Birkenau.

To Honor and to Remember

When she was 8 years old, Sally Wasserman was smuggled out of the Dombrowa Ghetto and hidden by two Polish Righteous Among the Nations, Eva and Mikolaj Turkin. She never saw her father, mother, and little brother again.

After the war, Sally was adopted by her aunt, her mother's sister, in Canada. It was not until 1998 that she read the last letter her mother wrote to her sister in Canada, from the Dombrowa Ghetto on July 22, 1943, before being deported to Auschwitz-Birkenau. Sally has shared her feelings about her mother and the contents of this last letter with thousands of students in many settings, including Auschwitz-Birkenau – the very place where her mother and little brother perished.

Sally tells students that before she discovered the letter and visited Poland, she resented her mother. "Why did my mother leave me behind? Why did she only take my little brother with her? Of course I understood my mother had saved me, but when I read the letter and visited the camps and stood in the gas chambers, that was the first time I felt the sacrifice of my mother and her courage and what her decision to give me up must have meant to her…. I no longer have resentment…now I have compassion and empathy for her. She was heroic, so courageous…. She had a strong belief that somehow, somewhere, regardless of the world she lived in there was some goodness. That's what I like to think."

Excerpts from the letter…

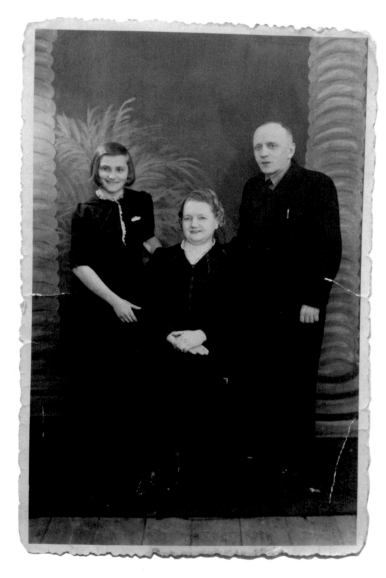

Eleven-year-old Sally in 1946, after the war, with her Polish rescuers, Eva and Mikolaj Turkin.

Dombrowa, July 22, 1943

My Dear Sister and Brother-in-Law,
I was able to leave my Sheindele (Sally) with Mr. Turkin. I met him only a few months ago.

He and his wife are very decent people, they took Sheindele under their care with love…I am writing this letter to you during the last days of my life. We are expecting death any time. We know what kind of death to expect. My dearest, the end is bitter and tragic.

I thank God for Mr. Turkin. I am sure he and his wife care for, and will save my child's life. I see the Angel of Death before me. I don't believe even a miracle can help us now. My little son Vovek and I are the last sacrificial victims. My dear ones, I write this letter with blood instead of ink. The only thing that makes it easier on my heart is knowing that Sheindele will be saved. She is in good hands with good people…. I can feel the pain in your hearts when you read this letter. It is not our fault. We are innocent, our future is lost and it cannot be changed…. It is terrible to die when your mind knows everything that is going to happen….

It hurts me terribly, it breaks my heart to have to write this letter to you, but you must know what happened to your family and how they disappeared. I am sorry to say that from that from the whole family, nobody is alive, we are the last. We are in danger and there is no possible way for us to live through this.

We do not have a way out. We are surrounded on all sides. I cannot write any more, I do not want to pain you. This is the last letter from me to you.

Your Sister Toby

A few days later Dombrowa was liquidated and declared *Judenfrei* (Jew free). Shortly thereafter Sally's mother and brother were murdered in Auschwitz.

Your Baby Survived, Mama

Robbie Waisman, 81-year-old Holocaust survivor, returned to his hometown of Skarzysko-Kamienna, Poland, with a group of high school students on the 2012 March of the Living.

"It took over 60 years before I found the courage to go back, to relive and to face these dark memories. I entered [my former home in the ghetto], my heart pounding, overcome with all the memories of long ago. I stopped, closed my eyes [and] I heard my Mom's beautiful voice saying to me, as she always did every night before I went to bed, '*Shluff Gesinter Hite*' (Sleep well), with a kiss and a hug. After a while I walked down the stairs to find all the teenagers who, I had thought, were waiting for me in the buses. There they were, all of them, keeping vigil, arm in arm, awaiting me in the courtyard – a wall of support to help me deal with all those thoughts, emotions, and memories.

"Next, together, we proceeded to find the site of the Synagogue, in Skarzysko. It was demolished...only two crumbling brick walls left. I said Kaddish again for my beloved Mom [murdered] in Treblinka where I found the Skarzysko monument."

Supported by a fellow survivor, Robbie looked upward and proclaimed: "I survived. I survived. Your baby survived, Mama." Then he burst into tears, embraced by the other survivors and surrounded by all of the children.

"I needed to go back after all these years to acknowledge to all my loved ones that I, the baby of the family, survived. I have no words to describe my love and respect for all of our young people, who joined from all over the world for the amazing March from Auschwitz to Birkenau."

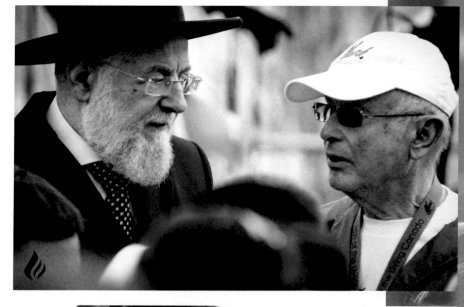

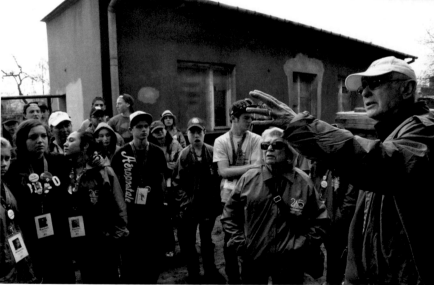

Top: Reuniting on the March of the Living with fellow survivor and Buchenwald inmate, Israel Meir Lau, later to become Chief Rabbi of Israel. Above and right: Robbie Waisman with students.

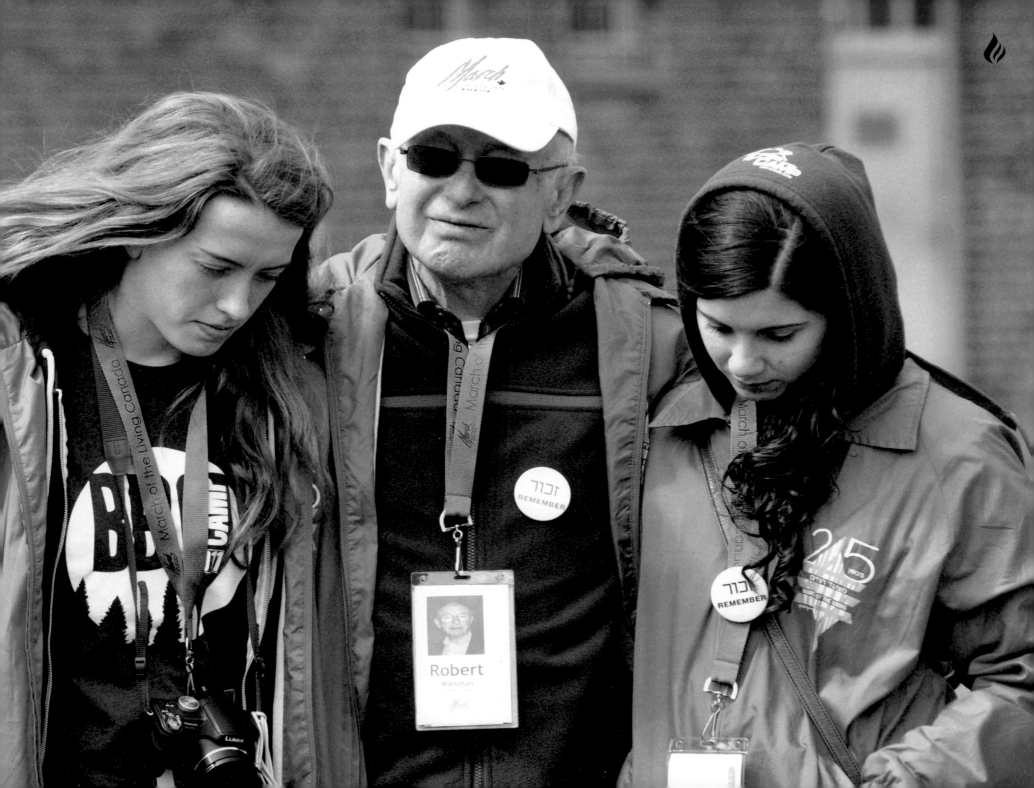

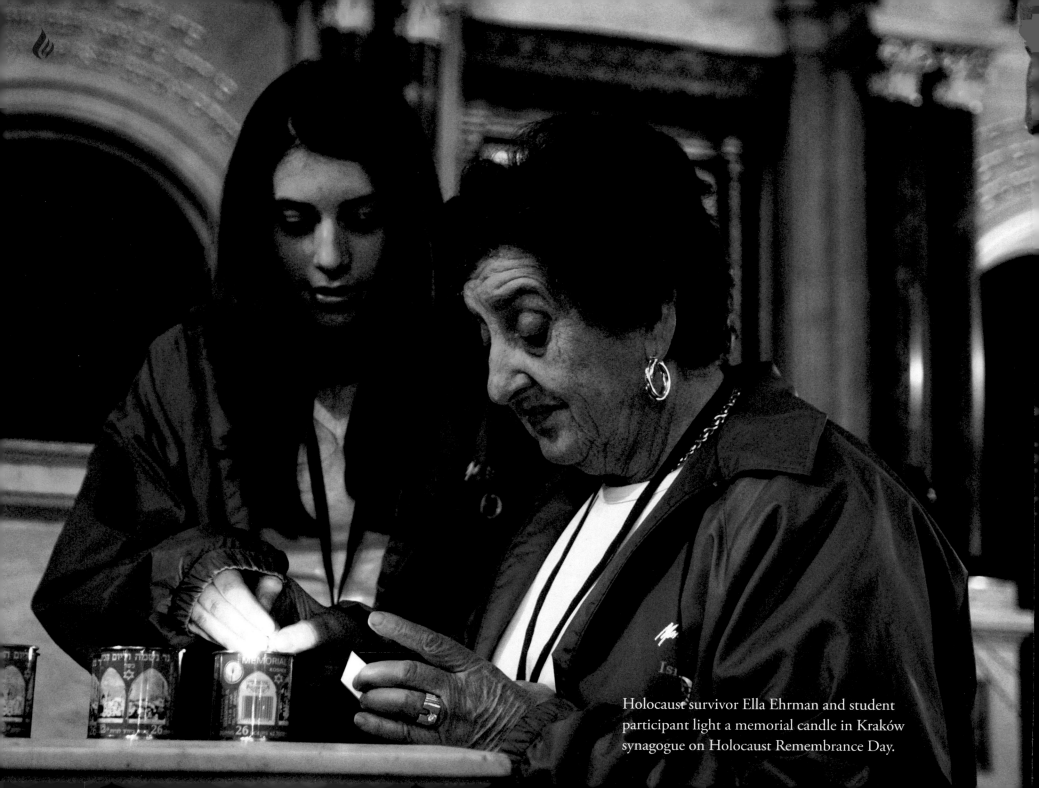

Holocaust survivor Ella Ehrman and student participant light a memorial candle in Kraków synagogue on Holocaust Remembrance Day.

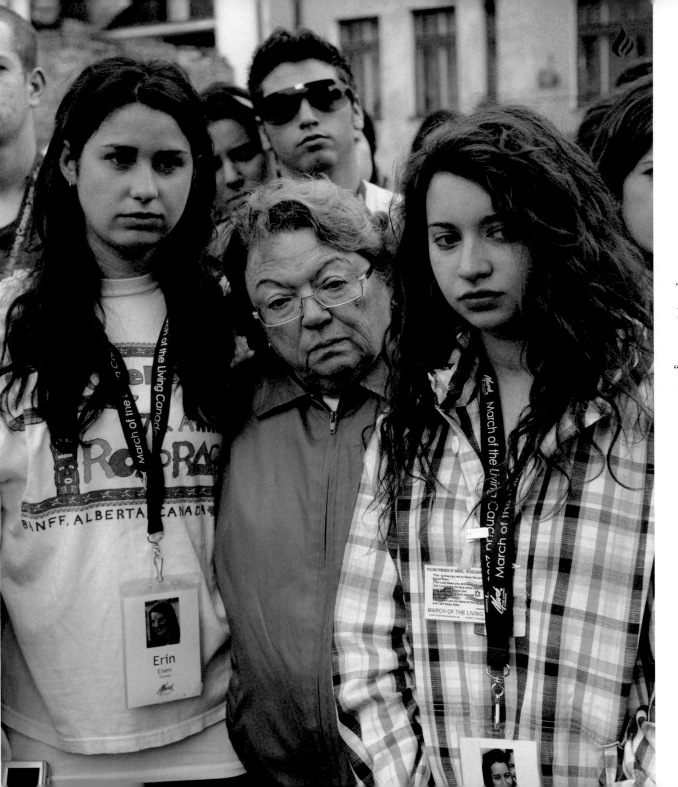

Hope for a Better Future

The interest shown by today's young people in studying the Holocaust is of great comfort to survivors like Anita Ekstein. "I have met and bonded with wonderful young people, and my hope is that they will never forget, and continue to remind the world when we survivors are no longer here. It gives us hope for a better future for the Jewish people and for all humanity."

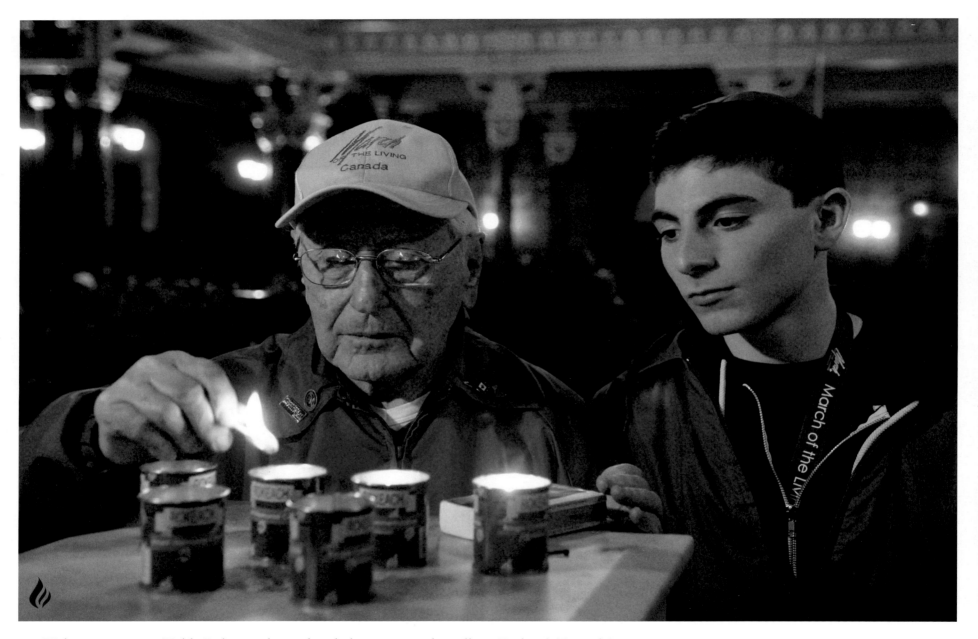

Holocaust survivor Teddy Bolgar and a student light a memorial candle in Kraków's Tempel Synagogue at the March of the Living Program on the eve of Holocaust Remembrance Day in 2010.

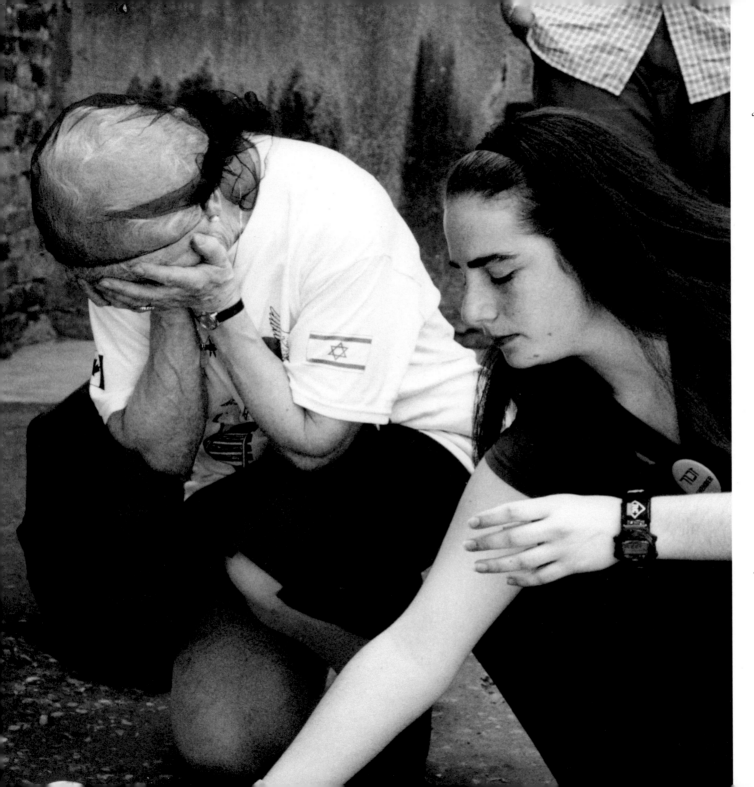

Her Last Words

"We arrived in Auschwitz July 19th, 1944. The minute we arrived [Dr. Josef] Mengele was there…. And, they separated us – and we didn't want to separate. They started kicking her. And I said, 'Go, Mommy, I don't want to see you suffer. Later on I'm going to see you.' But I never saw her any more. And always, always I remember her last words to me, 'Oh my dear, my glasses are in your pocket.' I said, 'Ok Mommy, I'm going to give you [them] back [later].'

"When I was back with the group of kids [on the March of the Living], we went to the museum in Auschwitz. We stepped into a room with glasses from the floor to the ceiling. I said, 'I'm sure… my mother's glasses are here, too.'"
—Eva Gelbman

A young March of the Living participant lights memorial candles at Auschwitz as Holocaust survivor Eva Gelbman remembers.

CHAPTER SIX

THE COMMITMENT OF A
NEW GENERATION OF WITNESSES

There is an old saying that maintains with the birth of every child, the world begins to hope anew. Each group of students returning home after spending time overseas, traveling with survivors, studying and learning from the history of genocide, reflects this optimistic notion.

In the applications submitted by many of the students, we see similar questions: What was the real nature of this terrible event? How could people act this way? And how could the world let them? Could it happen again? Are our own friends and neighbors capable of the same actions? Are we?

A second theme, also prevalent in the students' motivation, is this: It is not enough to study, to learn, and to read about the tragedies of the past. There is a need to examine the event in its place of origin, and to somehow begin to mend the world now, and to begin in the very place where the evil was perpetrated. This journey had to conclude on a note of hope.

In one extraordinarily memorable moment on the last day of one trip, a young man who had been silent most of the time revealed that, to his great shame, his grandfather had been a Nazi during WWII. Without hesitation, a young woman – a student he and the entire group knew was the granddaughter of three Holocaust survivors – rose up to comfort him.

"My intention," the young woman reflected later, "was to tell the young man this: 'Let's not bring prejudice into a new generation. I don't blame you for what your grandfather did. You are not your grandfather, and I don't blame you for his history. This is not your fault. You didn't do these things.'

"He was sobbing – so emotional. It was almost like a confession and I felt compelled to show him empathy and to absolve him of his guilt."

She then proceeded to hug him, as the entire circle of students applauded through their tears.

Indeed the students on this trip are not only studying history, they are also repairing history, creating and shaping a new future together, one where the grandchildren of perpetrator and victim embrace one another in a startling contrast to the murderous dynamic that existed on the very soil barely a few generations ago.

The questions, the doubts, the need to confront the evil and to somehow overcome it through a demonstrated allegiance to life, were the prevailing sentiments evinced from the students who have participated in these trips.

As one student wrote:

THE FIRE WITHIN ME
The fire in which my feelings burn is forever growing stronger. This trip represents more than the sites at which millions perished. It means life, hope, dreams, and the future. Being a part of this future, I wish to experience the past.
When the wind ceases to blow,
When the trees refuse to grow.
When the mountains no longer touch the sky,
And the stars do not shine bright.
That is when the children cease to remember Kristallnacht.
As the children of the future
As the hope our mothers bore
We must learn of the horrors past
To prevent the world from more.
—Robyn Hochglaube, March of the Living, 1992

One of the responses to the Holocaust might be that the human experiment is a failure, given the depravity of human conduct in this era. On pilgrimages to Holocaust and genocide sites in Europe, the students deny this conclusion by recommitting themselves to the concept of universal dignity and by valuing the human rights of all members of the human family.

The students uniformly reflect the conviction that the course of history can indeed be changed. As one African-American student wrote upon her return from the March of Remembrance and Hope, "They say that history repeats itself, as if that is an unchangeable reality. But the truth is, history does not repeat itself – it is people who repeat the mistakes of the past. But they don't have to and we don't have to!"

A student of Polish background, Bart Bonikowski, after listening to survivors on the trip, wrote:

> "I came to realize that…we must listen; we must welcome opportunities to become exposed to other cultures and to other peoples; and we must educate each other. Hope can only be realized through mutual understanding. Only through such an understanding can we promote knowledge and diminish hatred. And then maybe, just maybe, will we be able to say 'never again.'"

And from a Muslim student, Ayesha Siddiqua Chaudhry, when she returned:

> "I think the trip to Poland…forced us all to transcend our religious, political, and cultural boundaries in order to bear witness to the common humanity we all share. This common humanity is what should unite us when injustice is inflicted upon any one of us."

Finally, it is worth quoting African-American student Marie Mirlande Noel, who, in a speech at the United Nations on January 27, 2008, after she came back from Europe, said:

> "I challenge you, as I challenge myself, to be a beacon of change and to dare to question any inhumane treatment of others. I know that we cannot take care of all the world's injustices, but I urge you to at least identify one step that you can take toward making a positive difference, however small. This is how change begins."

Today, there is a generation of young people who are returning to their communities, to their universities, churches, temples, mosques, sweat lodges, synagogues, and other places of worship and meaning with one message: We can, we must, and we will do better.

These young people have matured into leaders in their own right, advocating for human dignity and compassion in a myriad of ways – founding organizations on campus to speak out against genocide and human rights abuses abroad, fighting against discrimination, intolerance, and injustice in their own countries, and teaching the children of the next generation about what they have learned on their journeys.

These students have fiercely committed themselves to changing the world in which we live.

Many already have.

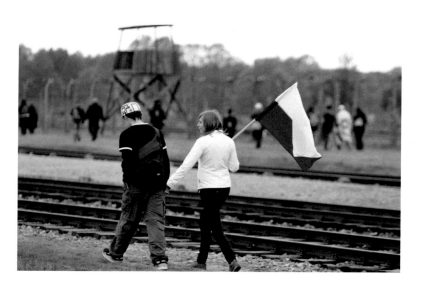

Polish students carry the Polish flag on railroad tracks in Auschwitz-Birkenau. Polish students make up one of the largest delegations on the March of the Living.

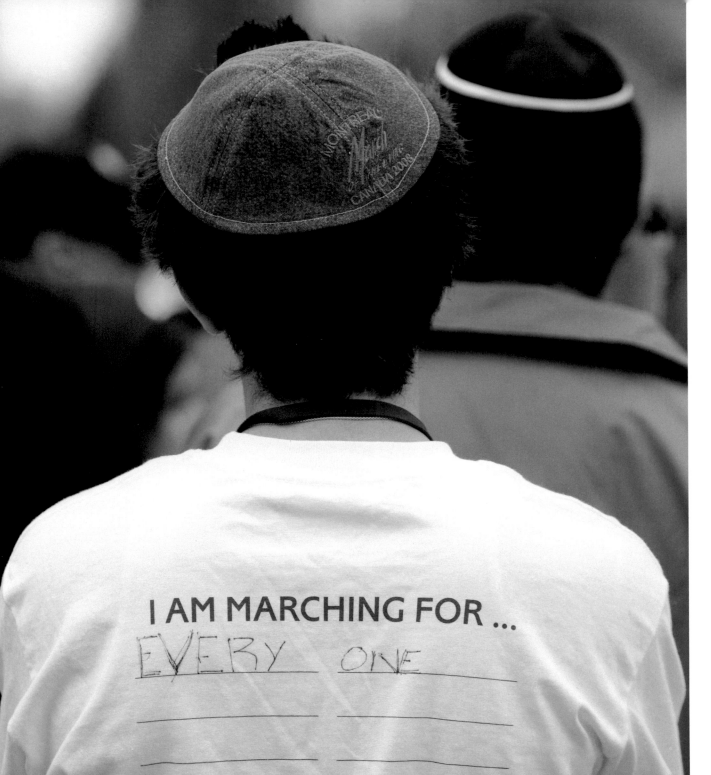

Students on the March are asked to choose a victim of the Holocaust for whom they will march. This student has chosen to march for all victims.

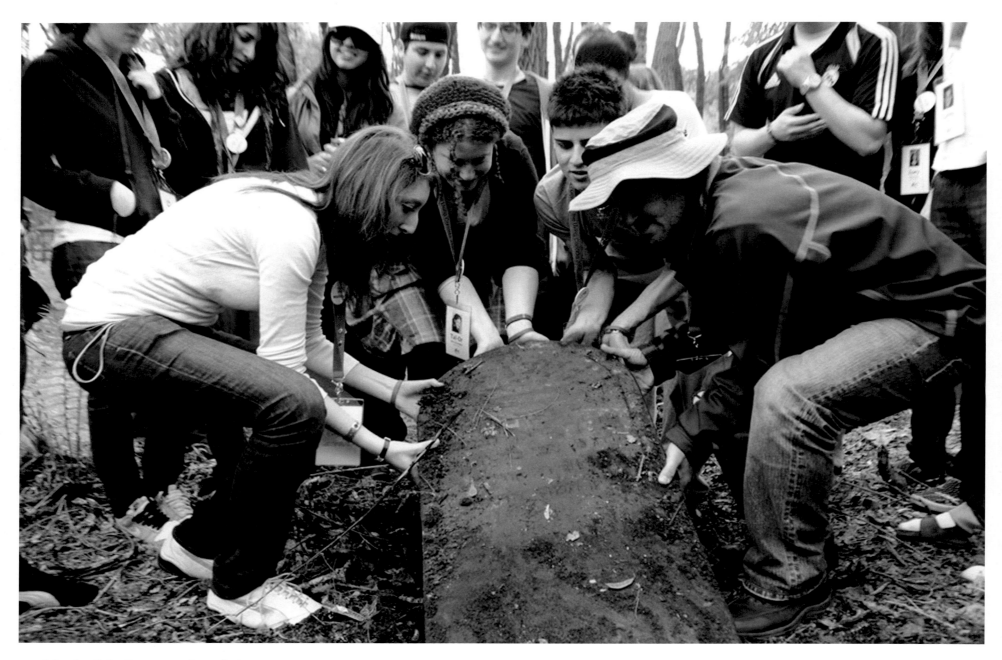

March of the Living students help restore
an abandoned cemetery in Poland.

ALL I CAN DO
I want to hug that person, but all I will feel is a gravestone.
I want to return it upright, but the stone stands crooked.
History stays put and all I can do is remember.
—Marni Levitt, 15, March of the Living, 1990

I felt a deep sense of loss in Poland; a loss in humanity for
the sacredness of life. My faith in the human race
deteriorated a little more with each death camp we visited.
[But] my deep sense of loss was accompanied by
something greater; something that restored my faith.
It was accompanied by hope [which I found] in my fellow
participants. Each of my companions has a gift of giving
me the ability to attempt to make a difference.... The camp
[Auschwitz-Birkenau] that was once run by savage murderers was now overcome
by people who condemned such acts of evil. This gave me hope that one day we
shall overcome. I hope that it does the same for you.
—Trisha Lynn Cowie, Irish-Ojibway Canadian, March of Remembrance and Hope

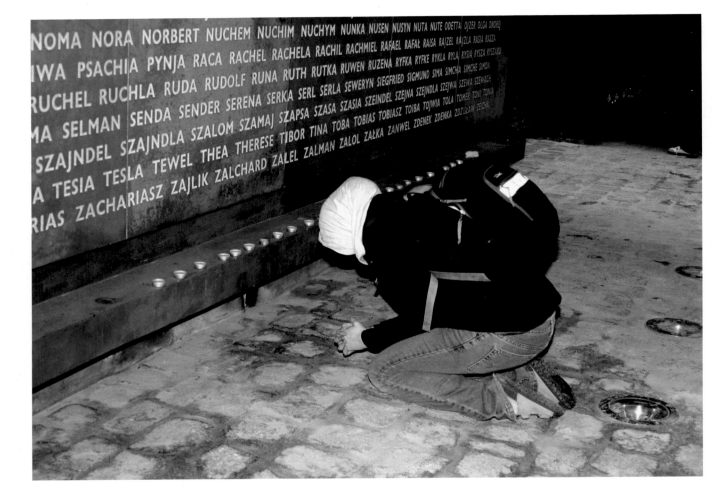

The Belzec death camp memorial
moved this student to kneel in prayer.

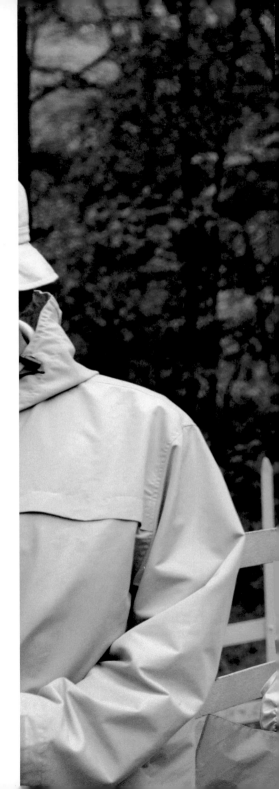

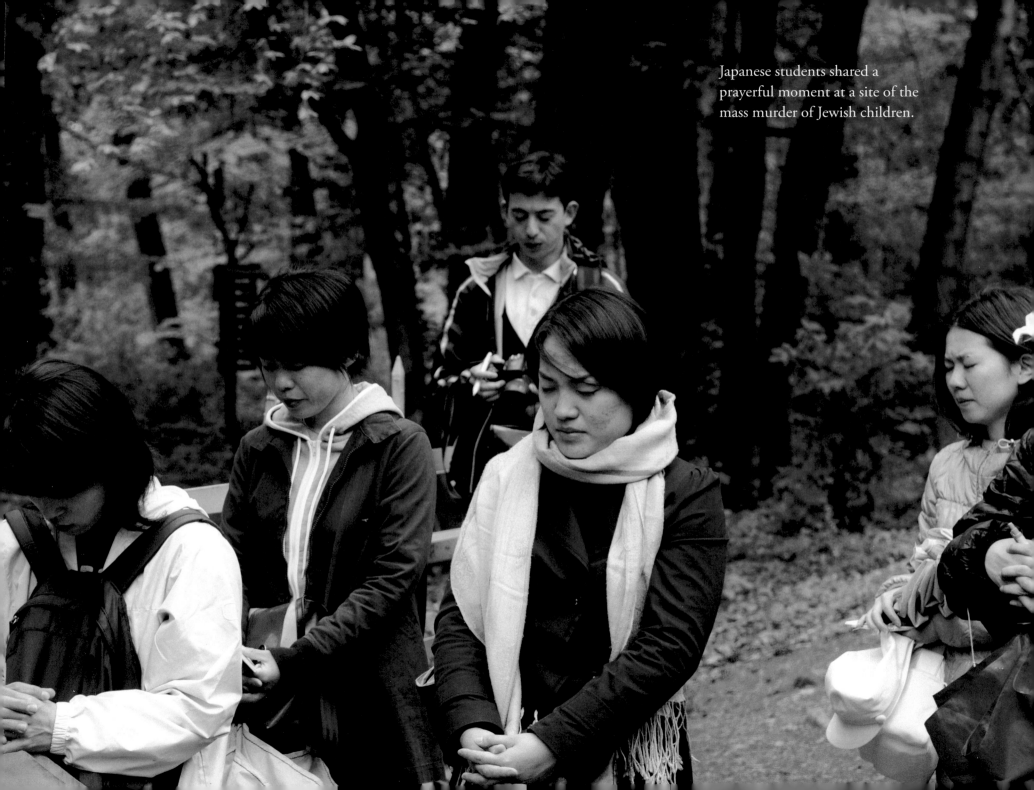

Japanese students shared a prayerful moment at a site of the mass murder of Jewish children.

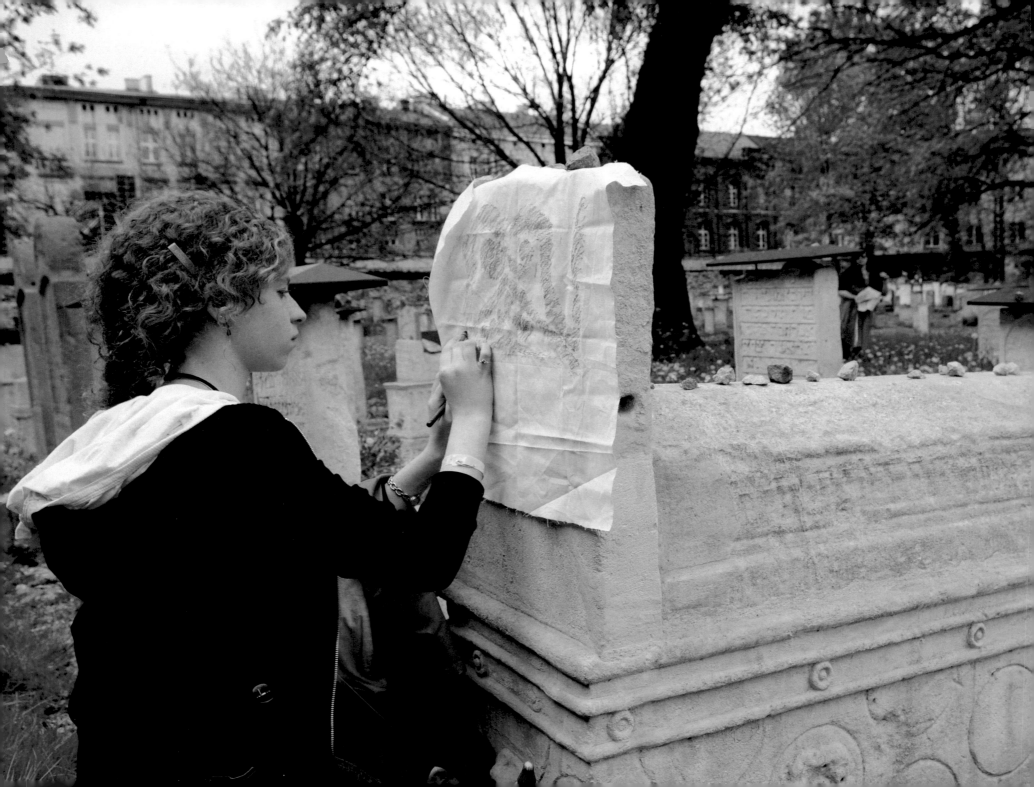

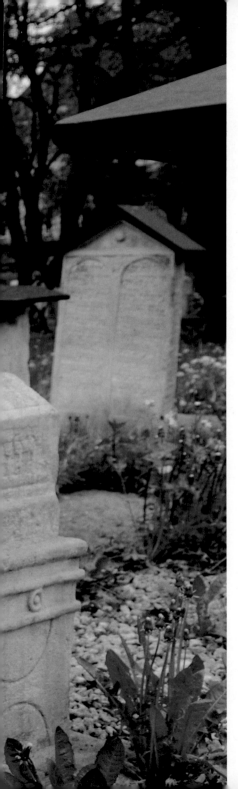

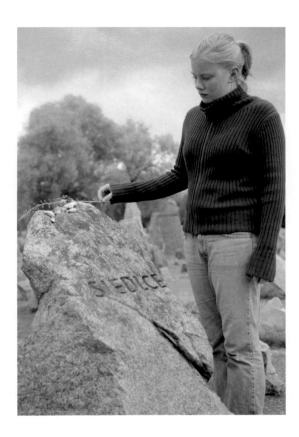

A somber student places a flower on the Treblinka memorial stone for the town of Siedlce. Some 10,000 of the town's Jews were murdered at Treblinka in August 1942.

A student participant traces the inscription on a tombstone at Remuh cemetery in Kraków, established in 1532.

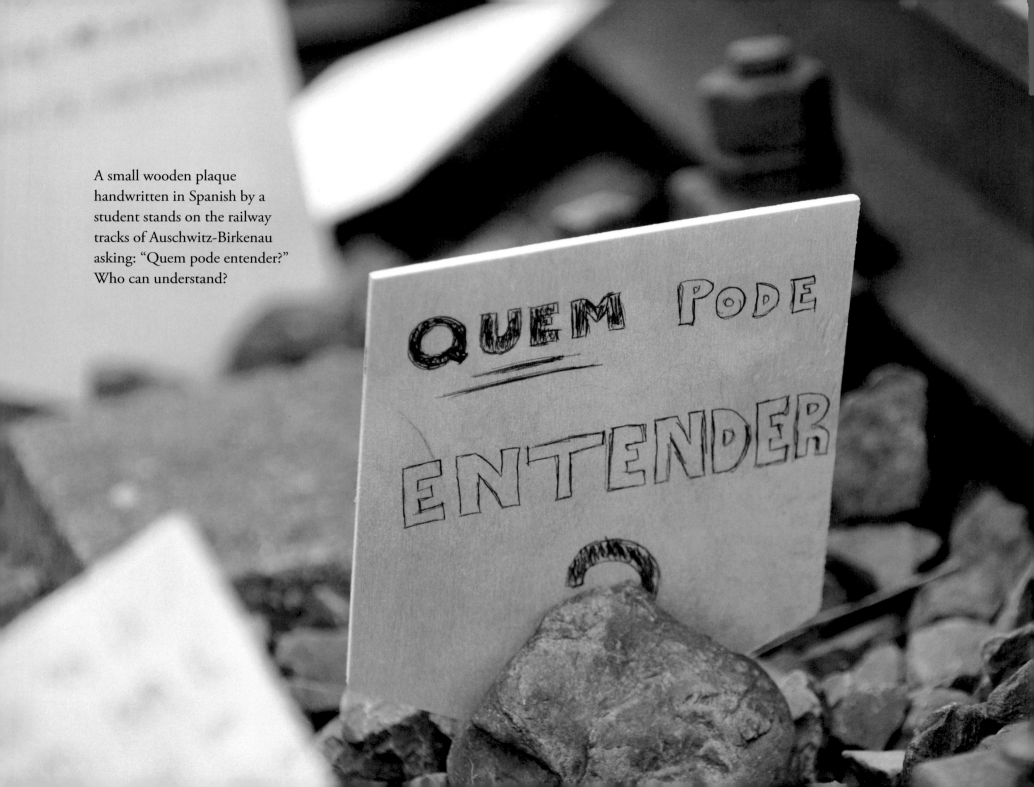

A small wooden plaque handwritten in Spanish by a student stands on the railway tracks of Auschwitz-Birkenau asking: "Quem pode entender?" Who can understand?

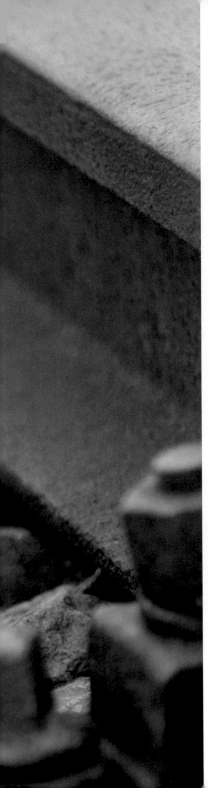

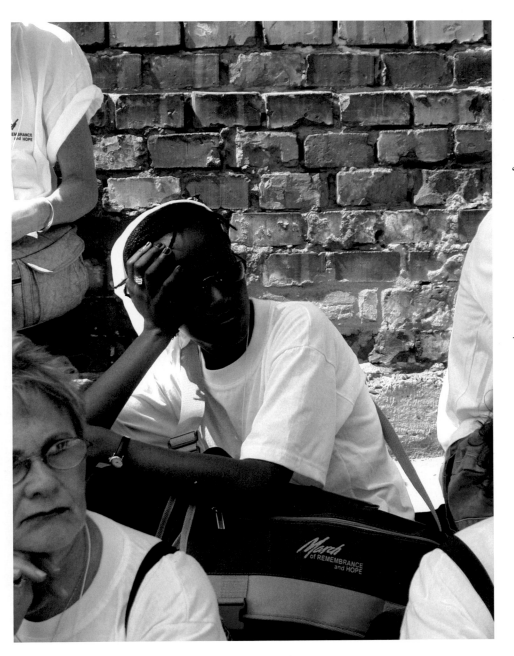

Hitler Can be Defeated

"When a survivor of the Holocaust holds hands with a Rwandan student in Auschwitz, and when they dry each other's tears and learn from one another, we know that Hitler and tyrants like him can be defeated."
—Juliet Karugahe

Juliet Karugahe, survivor of the Rwandan Genocide visiting Auschwitz-Birkenau on the March of Remembrance and Hope.

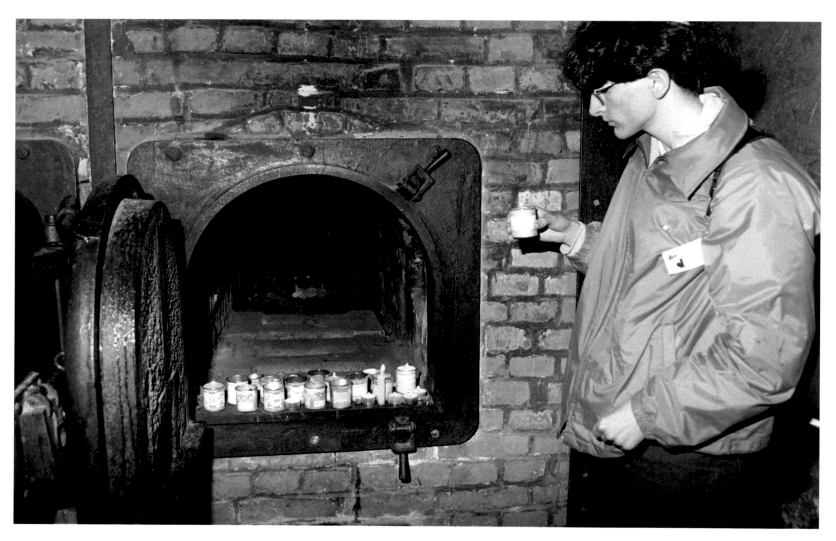

Memorial candles at the crematoria of
Auschwitz-Birkenau flicker in remembrance
of the people murdered there.

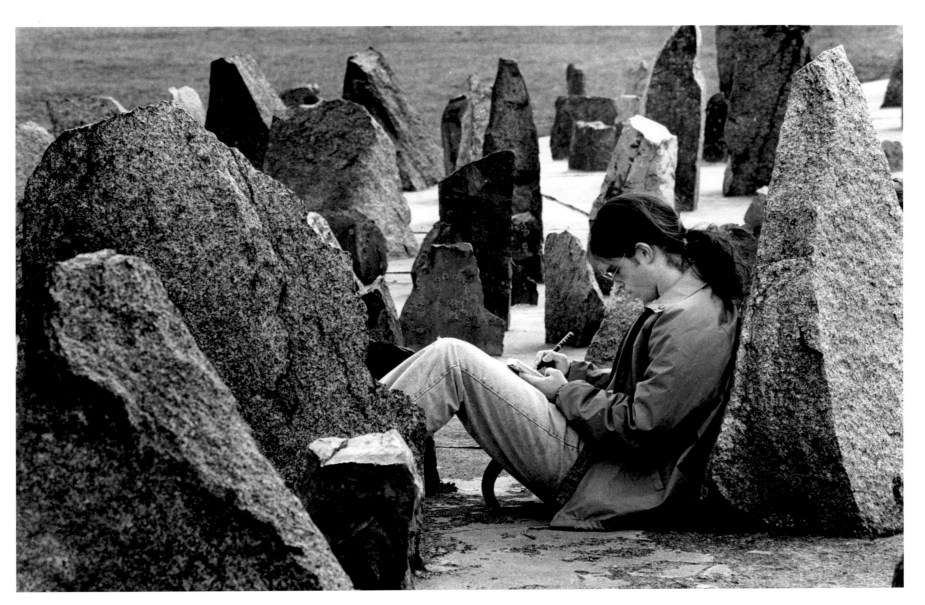

Amid the stones of the Treblinka death camp
memorial, reflections recorded in a diary speak of
the profound effects of the March of the Living.

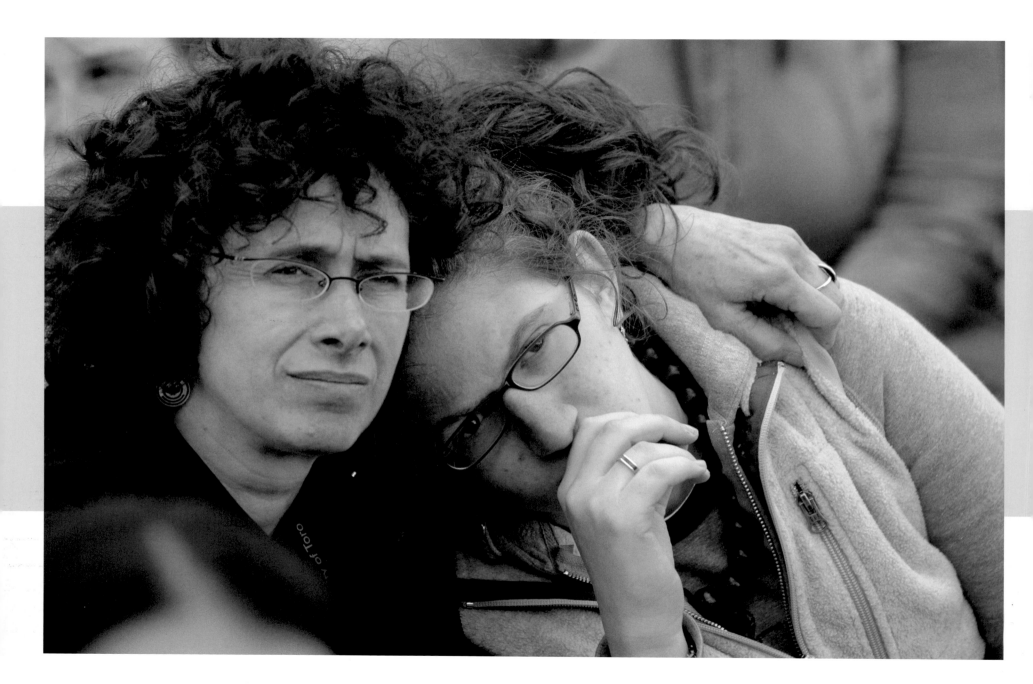

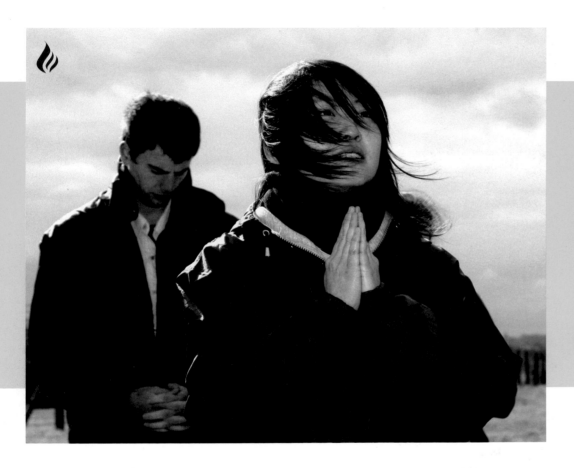

FACES OF THE MARCH

They come from many countries, many cultures, many faiths to stand moved and shaken at the sites of humanity's great failure. They leave as one, a young generation committed to remembering, ready to keep watch, determined to create a better future.

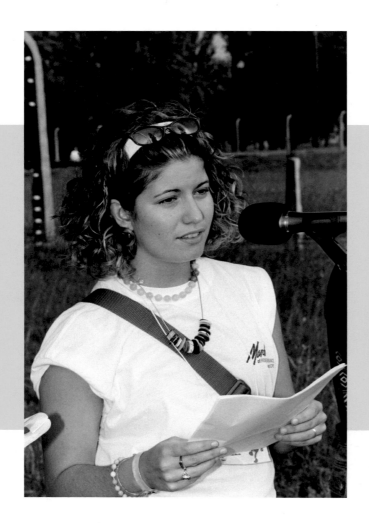

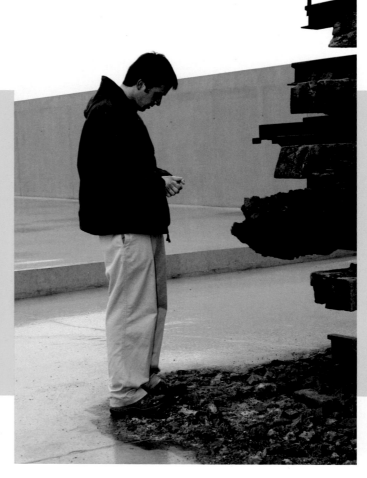

116

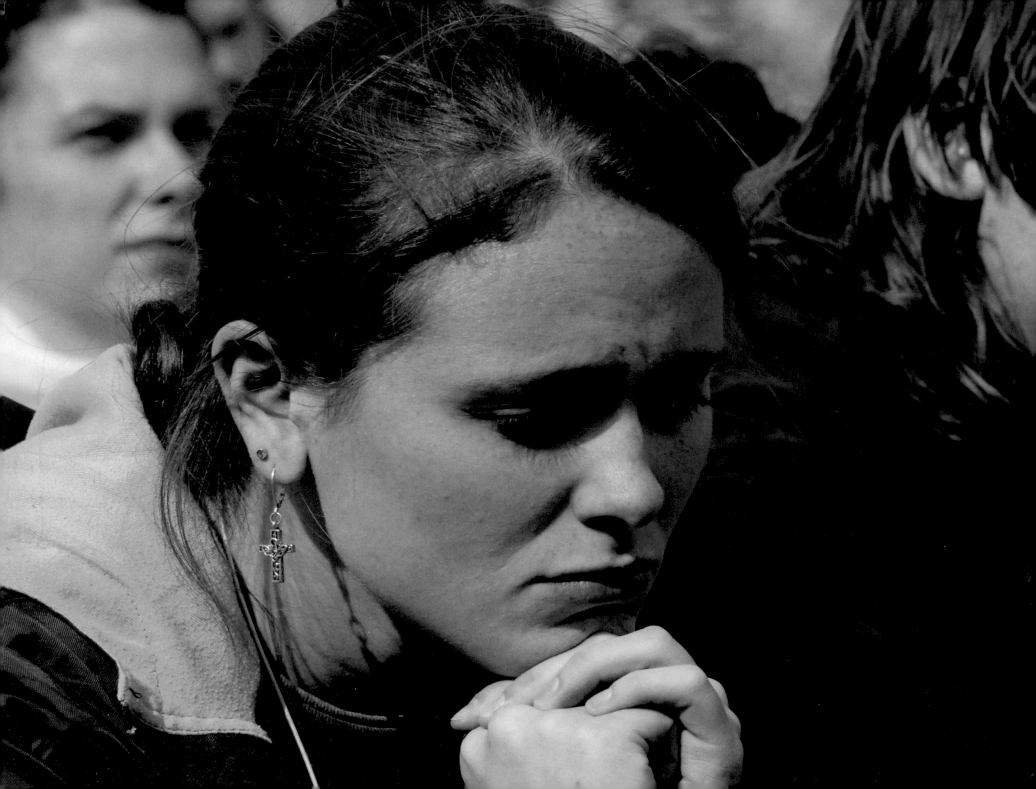

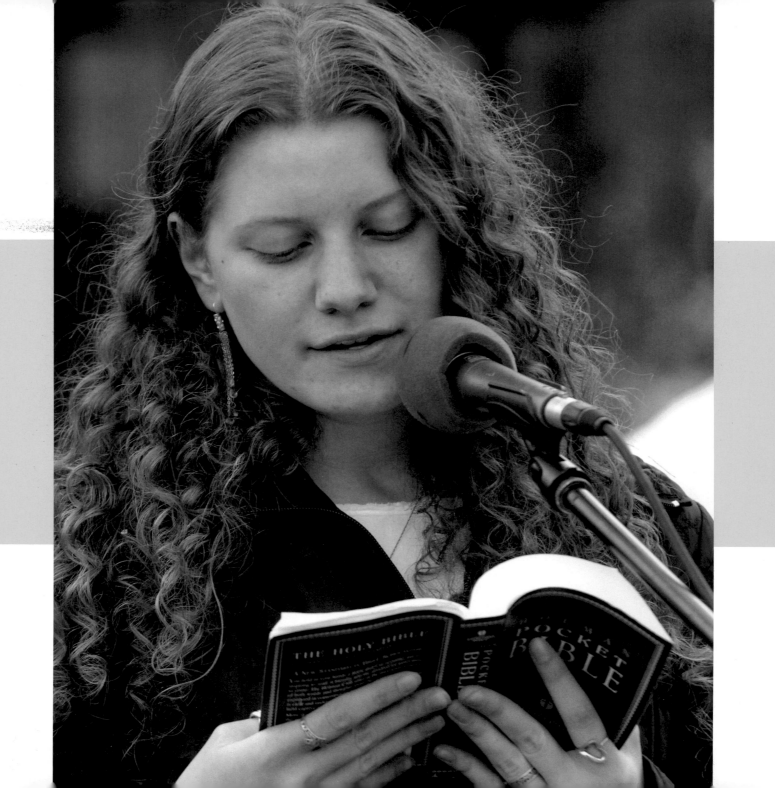

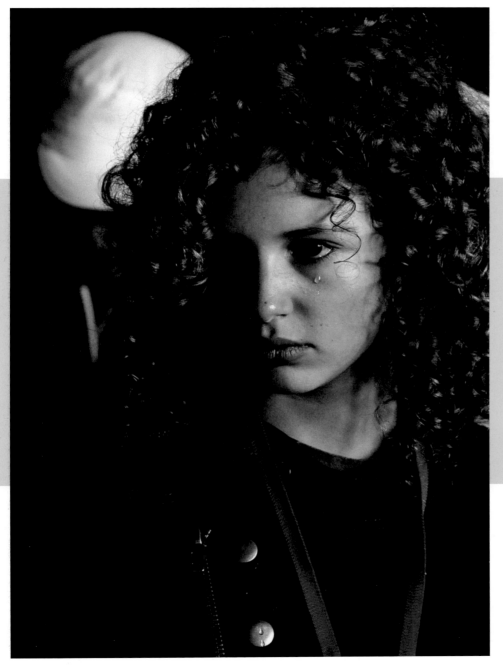

Although there were tears
in everyone's eyes,
there was in every heart, a flame
burning with hope for the future,
and the strength and will to never let
a tragedy like this ever happen again
to anyone...
—Shauna Zelig,
March of the Living, 1990

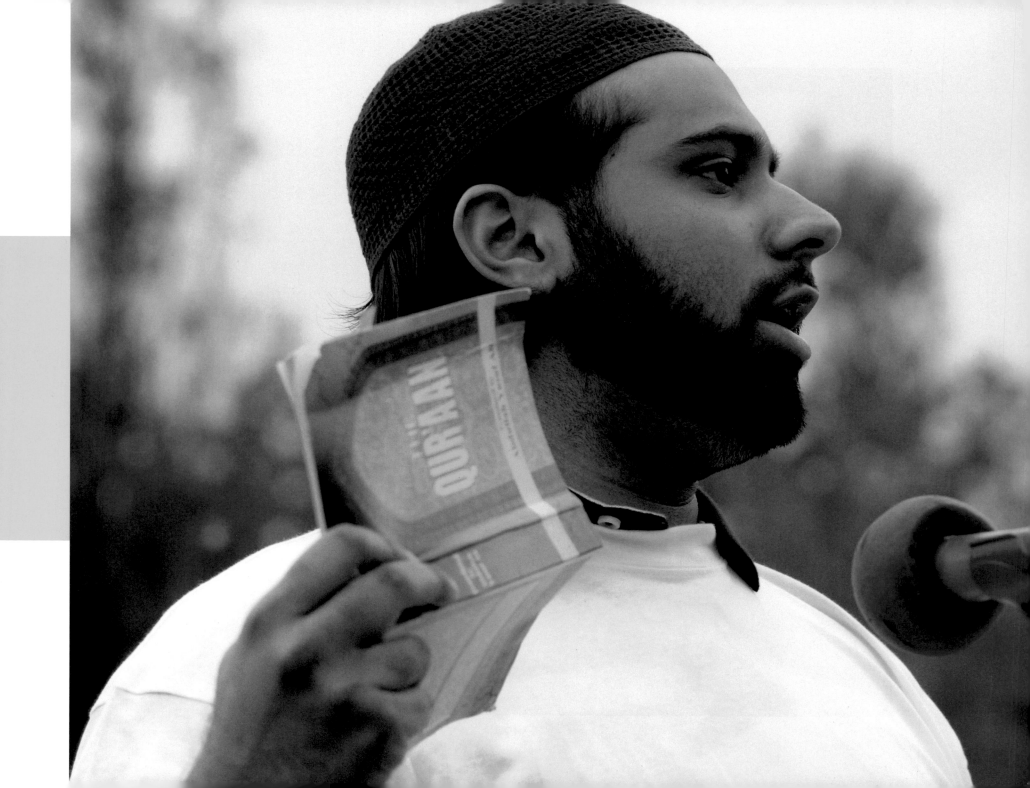

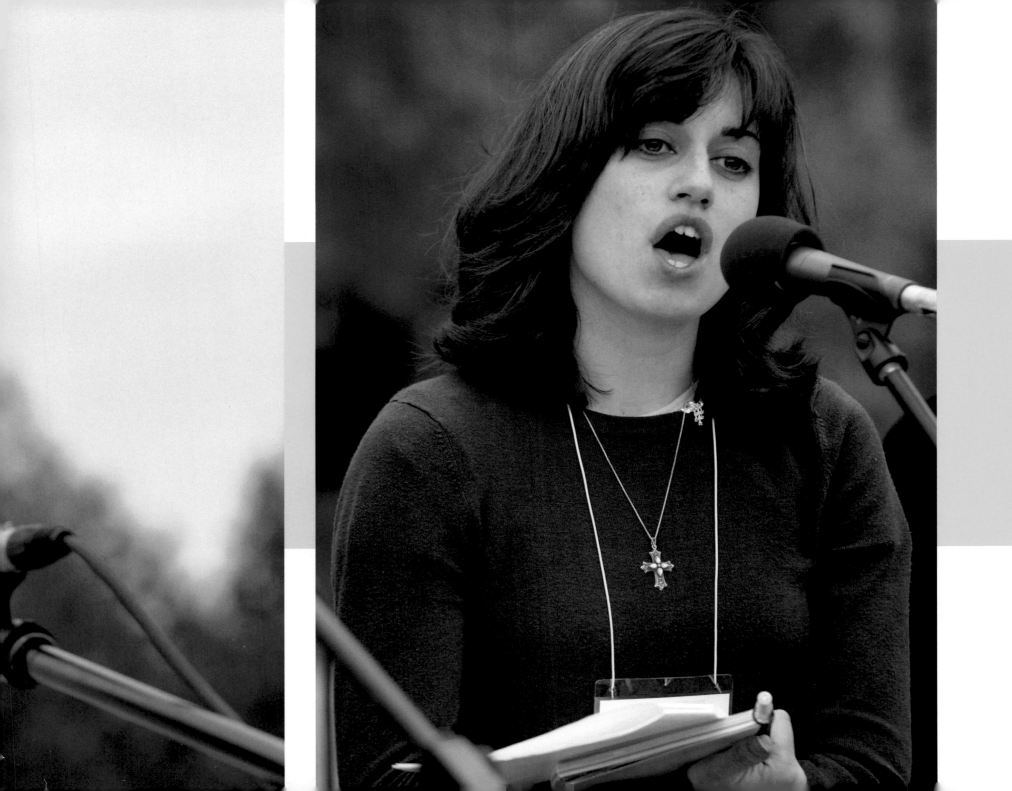

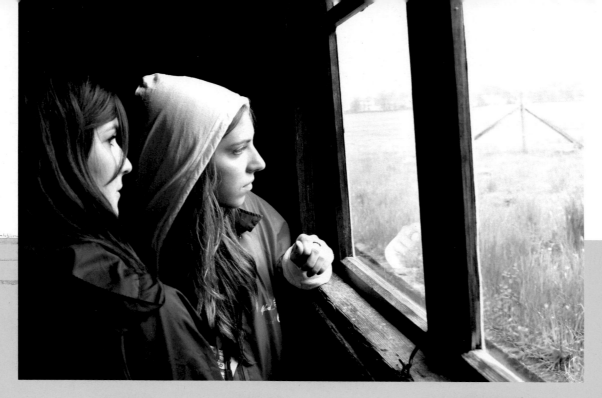

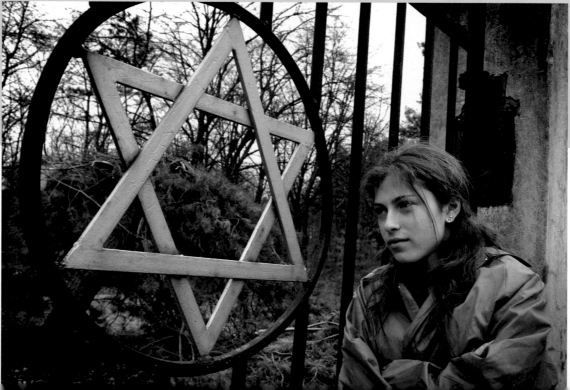

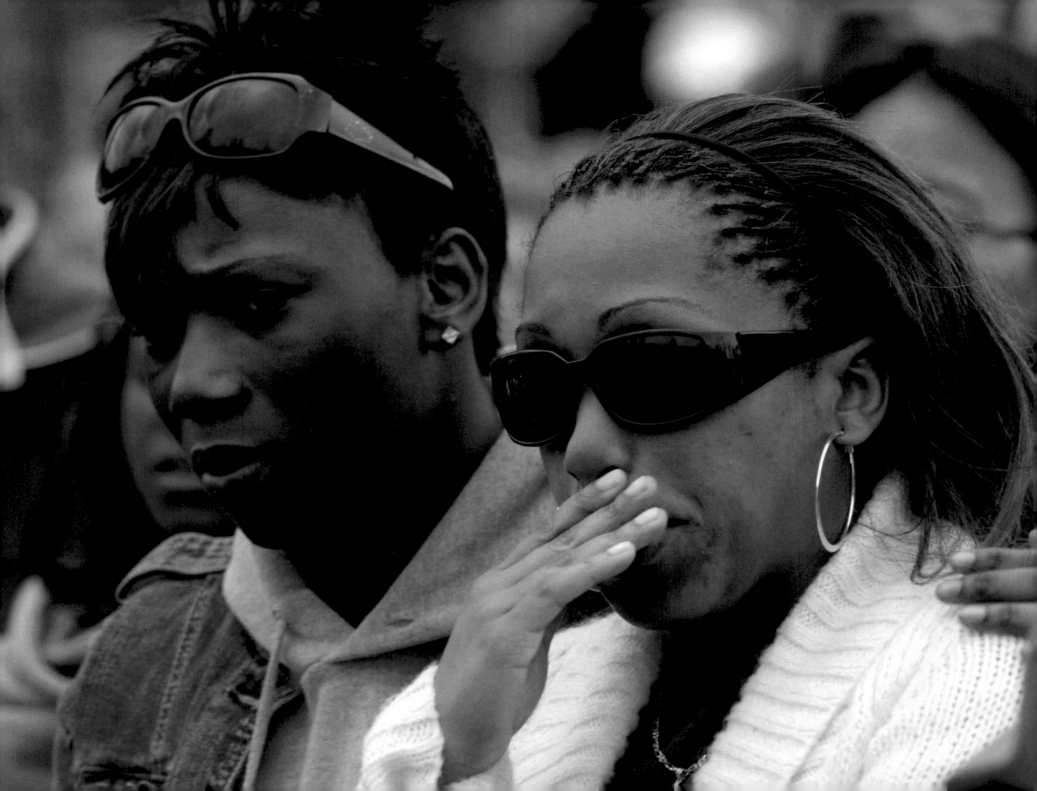

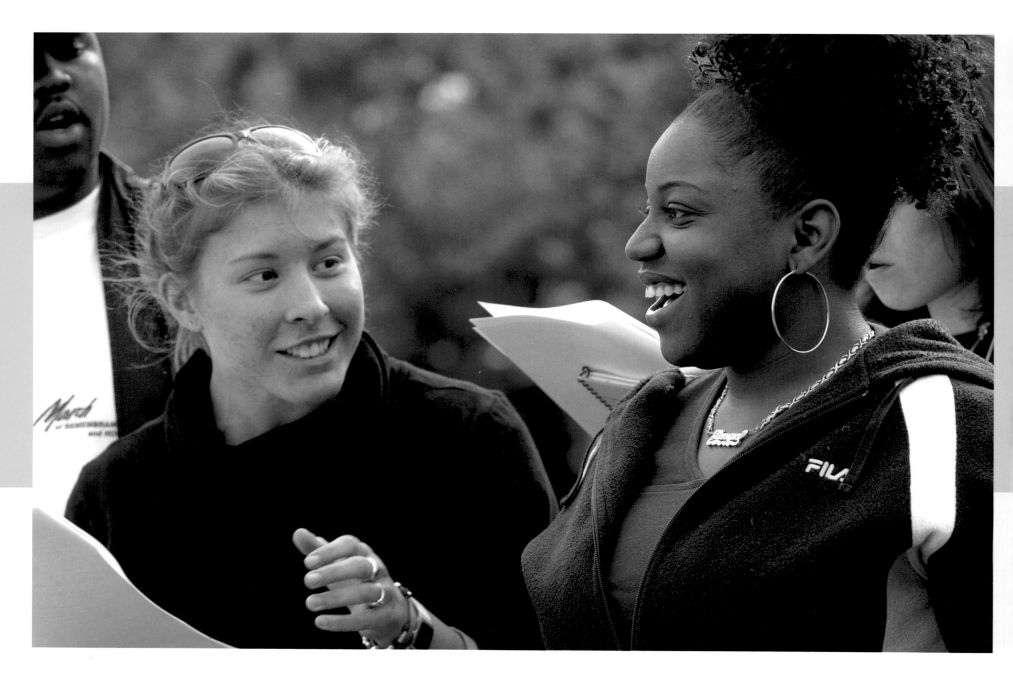

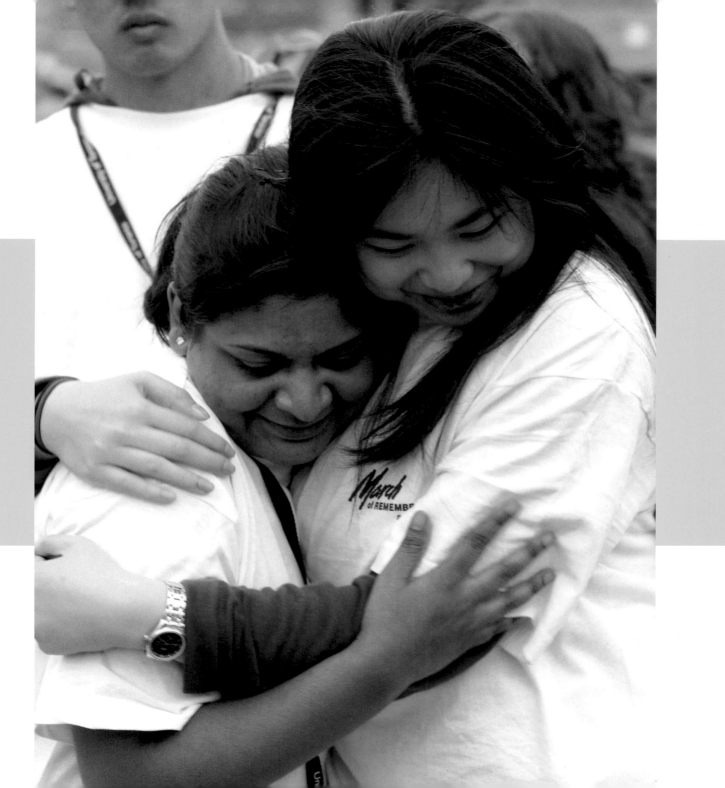

THE MARCH

The March of the Living serves as a hopeful counterpoint to the Death Marches when hundreds of thousands of Jews and other innocent victims were forced by the Nazis to cross vast expanses of European terrain under the harshest of conditions.

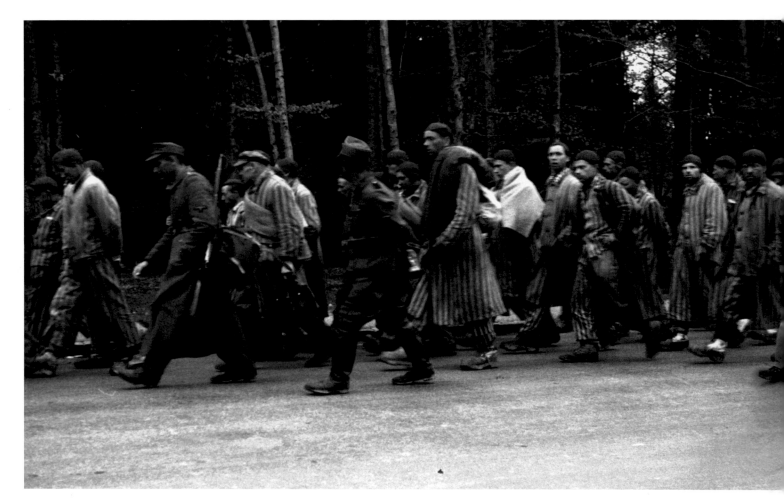

Death March at Grünwald, close to Munich, on April 29, 1945.

OF THE LIVING

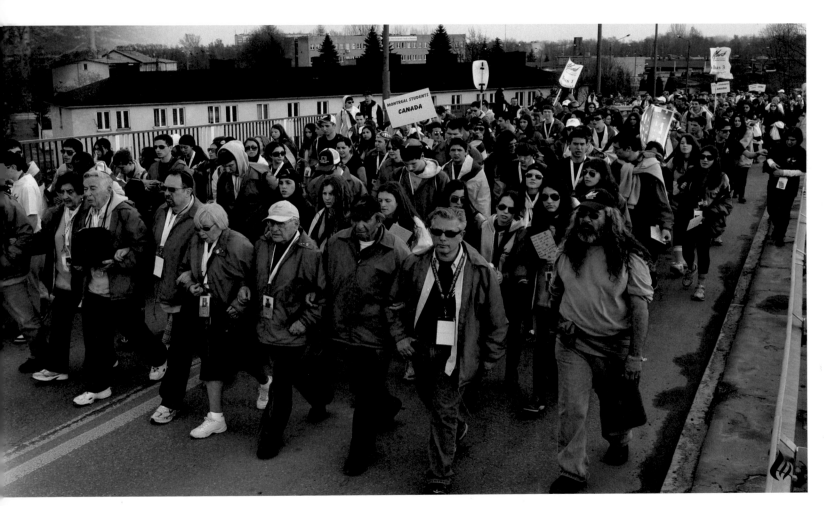

On Holocaust Remembrance Day, thousands of March of the Living participants, including many survivors, march silently, hand in hand, from Auschwitz to Birkenau, the largest Nazi concentration camp complex built during World War II.

In our blue jackets we marched as one, marched against dehumanization, marched against the past, marched toward the future...
—Debbie Roth, March of the Living participant

AND STILL I CANNOT HATE
I see bones and hair, shoes and glasses.
While in a Nazi hell ruled by the devil's brother,
But still I cannot hate.

I see women's brushes, men's talisim and babies' tattered clothing,
But still I cannot hate.

I see splintered boards where people laid their weary bodies,
I see where people slaved and tried to exist,
And still I cannot hate.
I see the death and destruction,
But still I cannot hate.

I won't continue this tragedy, I won't spread the disease.
I won't fan the flames, that hate like this inspires.
—Jennifer Staffenberg, 17, March of the Living, 1994

Acknowledgments

Portions of book based on United Nations Exhibit, "When you Listen to a Witness You become a Witness," Created by Eli Rubenstein and Lara Silberklang; Designed by Sara Jaskiel; Chief Advisor and Associate Creator: Dr. David Machlis; Academic Advisor: Dr. David Silberklang

Photographic Credits

Nir Bareket (112, 113), Eli ben Boher (60, 78, back cover top left), Jacek Bendarczyk/EPA (79), Sergey Bermeniev (13), Ryan Blau (cover, 22, 23, 65, 86, 94, 114, 122 top, 127, back cover top right), Lior Cohen (71, left), Jesse Gold (58), Rosemary Goldhar (31, 32, 33, 68, 82, 97, 106, 108, 116 left, 122, bottom), Naomi Harris (76), Igal Hecht (52, 83, 85), Adele Lewin (77), Dafna Lorber (21, 26, 111), Moshe Milner (88), Katka Reszke (49), Emmanuel Santos (28), Michael Soberman (81), David Sondervan (55), Manuel F. Sousa (104), Monique de St. Croix (89, 92-93), Dominique Teoh (67), Elad Winkler (42, 90), Yonatan Zaid (51 right), Yossi Zeliger (20, 24, 30, 38, 46, 50, 51 left, 53, 54, 59, 62, 66, 70, 71 right, 80, 84, 95, 96, 102, 103, 106, 107, 108, 109, 110, 112, 113, 114, 115, 116 right, 117, 118, 119, 120, 121, back cover bottom left and right)

Archival Photo Credits

Yad Vashem (12, 41 Anne Frank, 13, 126)
United States Holocaust Memorial Museum (10, 11)
United States Holocaust Memorial Museum,
courtesy of Beit Hannah Senesh (41)
Tomek Steppa (41 Krystyna Wituska)
Sally Wasserman (91)

Map

Francois Blanc, Banff Technologies (19)

Additional Book Credits

For You Who Died I Must Live On: Reflections on the March of the Living, Eli Rubenstein (ed.), Mosaic Press, 1993
Liberating the Ghosts: Photographs and Texts from the March of the Living, Raphael Shevelev and Karen Schomer, Lenswork Publishing, 1996

Special Thanks to the March of the Living International Board of Directors

Dr. Shmuel Rosenman, Chairman
Baruch Adler, Maude Dahme, Rabbi Yochanan Fried, Shlomo Grofman, Phyllis Greenberg Heideman, Dr. Ralph Madeb, Moshe Punsky, Scott Saunders

March of the Living International Staff

Executive Staff: Yossi Kedem, Dr. David Machlis, Aharon Tamir
Support Staff: Liz Sinnreich Panitch, Naomi Sion

Survivors, Righteous Among the Nations & Liberators Featured

Trudy Album (89), Asher Aud (88), Halina Birenbaum (70), Teddy Bolgar (96), Lillian Boraks-Nemetz (77), Rick Carrier (Liberator, 54), Judy Weissenberg Cohen (76), Irving Cymbler (59), Elie Dawang (back cover, top right), Mickey Dorsey (Liberator, 52, 53), Ella Ehrmann (94), Ernest Ehrmann (65), Max Eisen (68), Anita Ekstein (33, 95), Anna Heilman of blessed memory (26), Eva Gelbman (97), Max Glauben (60, back cover, top left), Bill Glied (85), Sylvia Ruth Gutman (66, 80), Pinchas Gutter (62), Max Iland (81), Olga Koss (51), Jerzy Kozminski of blessed memory (Righteous Among the Nations, 46), Bronka Krygier of blessed memory (42-43), Stanislaw & Zygmunt Krynski (Righteous Among the Nations, 48-49), Rabbi Israel Meir Lau (92), Miles Lerman of blessed memory (33), Nate Leipciger (71, 82, 83), Faigie Libman (58), Frank Lowy (67), Krystyna Puchalski-Maciejewskai (Righteous Among the Nations, 50), Joe Mandel (52), Hilbert Margol (Liberator, 55) Irving Roth (54), Mayer Schondorf of blessed memory (84), Rena Schondorf (86), David Shentow (71), Eva and Mikolaj Turkin of blessed memory (Righteous Among the Nations, 91), Robbie Waisman (92-93), Sally Wasserman (90-91), Elie Wiesel (13), Czeslawa Zak (Righteous Among the Nations, 51), Miriam Zakrojczyk (51), Felix Zandman (50), Sidney Zoltak (48-49)

The testimonies of many of the survivors who appear in this book are available online at

March of the Living Digital Archives Project
http://molarchiveproject.com/ and
the USC Shoah Foundation Archives
https://sfi.usc.edu/search_the_archive
and by accessing the USC Shoah Foundation or the Digimarc digital watermarks on selected pages. Special thanks to BlueSoho for their dedicated work with this emerging technology.

March of the Living Digital Archives, a project of Jewish Federations Canada-UIA, has received funding from: Department of Citizenship & Immigration Canada - Multiculturalism Section, The Claims Conference, and Laura & Dennis Bennie.

Thank you to
Yad Vashem, the United States Holocaust Memorial Museum, Polin: The Museum of the History of Polish Jews, and the USC Shoah Foundation for their significant assistance. Also to Dr. David Silberklang for his patient and expert advice, and to Dr. Sharon Kangisser Cohen for her wise suggestions.

Additional Support
Alvin Abrams, Nancy Ditkofsky, Shira Gelkopf, Michael Hirsh, Linda Kislowicz, Roberta Malam, Ali Newpol, Dr. Karen Palayew, Sherri Rotstein, Alana Saxe, Ralph Shedletsky Michael Soberman, Sherrie Stalarow, Irene Tomaszewski, Shauna Waltman, Naomi Wise, Carla Wittes, Evan Zelikovitz

To all the staff at Second Story Press
Margie Wolfe, Publisher
Kathryn Cole and Carolyn Jackson, Editors
Melissa Kaita, Graphic Design
Thank you for your tireless effort and dedication in producing this book.

Special Note of Gratitude
Mordechai Ben-Dat and Christina Mairin

Thank you to the hundreds of thousands of people, young and old alike, survivors, teachers and students of all faiths and backgrounds, for embarking on this difficult and sacred pilgrimage and for your faith and belief that the world can – and indeed must – learn from this most tragic period of human history.